Go Network Mastery

The Path to Becoming a Network Programming Expert

Phillips Jeremy

Table of Contents

Preface

Hello! If you've picked up this book, chances are you're as excited about the power of networks and the elegance of Go as I am. Building network applications can feel like magic – connecting different systems, exchanging data, and creating experiences that span the globe. And Go, with its clean syntax, powerful concurrency features, and focus on performance, is the perfect language to bring that magic to life. This book is your guide to unlocking that potential and building high-performance network applications that are robust, scalable, and a joy to work with.

Background and Motivation

My own fascination with network programming started with a simple chat application. The feeling of connecting two computers and exchanging messages was exhilarating. As I explored further, I realized the immense possibilities of network applications, from web servers and APIs to distributed systems and real-time communication platforms. Go quickly became my language of choice for this domain. Its built-in concurrency made handling multiple connections a breeze, and its performance was simply outstanding. However, I noticed a gap: a lack of comprehensive resources specifically focused on building network applications with Go. That's what inspired me to write this book. I wanted to share my knowledge and passion, empowering others to build amazing things with Go and the power of networking.

Purpose and Scope

This book aims to be your one-stop guide to network programming in Go. We'll start with the fundamentals, making sure you have a solid understanding of networking concepts and how Go handles sockets, protocols, and data formats. From there, we'll progress to building practical applications, including client-server models, RESTful APIs, and real-time systems using WebSockets. We won't just cover the "how," but also the "why," explaining the design choices and best practices that lead to high-quality code. Finally, we'll explore advanced topics like security, performance optimization, testing, and deployment, equipping you with the skills to build production-ready network applications. While we'll cover a broad range of topics, the focus will always be on practical application and clear, concise explanations.

Target Audience

This book is written for developers who have some basic familiarity with Go. You don't need to be a networking expert to get started. If you're comfortable with Go's syntax, data types, and control structures, you're well on your way. Whether you're a seasoned programmer looking to add network programming to your toolkit, a student exploring the possibilities of distributed systems, or a hobbyist eager to build your next project, this book has something for you.

Organization and Structure

The book is structured in three parts. Part I lays the groundwork, covering the essential networking concepts and Go's core networking capabilities. Part II dives into building applications, exploring client-server architectures, concurrency, APIs, and WebSockets. Part III focuses on advanced topics, including security, performance optimization, testing, and deployment. Each chapter builds upon the previous one, creating a smooth learning experience. Throughout the book, you'll find plenty of code examples, illustrations, and exercises to reinforce your understanding.

Invitation to Read

I'm truly excited for you to begin this exploration of network programming with Go. I believe that by the end of this book, you'll have the knowledge and confidence to build robust, high-performance network applications. So, grab your favorite editor, get your Go environment set up, and let's get started! I hope you find this book informative, engaging, and most importantly, helpful in your journey to becoming a Go network master. Let's build something amazing!

Chapter 1: Introduction to Networking Concepts

Welcome to the exciting world of network programming! Before we jump into writing Go code, it's essential to understand the fundamental concepts that underpin how networks function. Think of this chapter as your friendly introduction to the backstage workings of the internet. We'll explore the key models, protocols, and ideas that make communication between computers possible.

1.1 The OSI Model

Let's explore the OSI model, a cornerstone of network understanding. It's not a protocol itself, but rather a conceptual framework—a way to organize and visualize the complex processes involved in network communication. Think of it as the architect's blueprint for how data travels across a network. It divides the process into seven distinct layers, each with specific responsibilities, making it much easier to grasp the overall picture and troubleshoot network issues.

The OSI model isn't about specific technologies or implementations; it's about the *functions* involved in communication. It's a reference point, a common language for network professionals. While the TCP/IP model is what's actually used on the internet, understanding the OSI model provides a solid foundation for understanding networking concepts in general.

Let's walk through each layer, starting from the bottom, the one closest to the physical hardware

The Physical Layer

This layer is the bedrock of network communication. It's concerned with the raw transmission of data as electrical, optical, or radio signals. It defines the physical characteristics of the transmission medium—the cables, connectors, signal voltages, frequencies, and so on. Think of it as the electrician's domain: setting up the wiring, ensuring the correct voltage, and making sure the signals can travel across the wire. This layer doesn't interpret the meaning of the bits; it simply transmits them. Specifications like Ethernet cable types (Cat5e, Cat6), fiber optic cable specifications, and connector types (RJ-45, SC) all fall under the Physical Layer. For example, the physical layer specifies how a '1' is represented as a voltage level and a '0' as the absence of that voltage.

The Data Link Layer

Building upon the Physical Layer, the Data Link Layer adds structure to the raw bits. It organizes them into *frames*, which are essentially packets of data with added header and trailer information. This layer is responsible for reliable communication between two directly connected devices. It handles error detection and correction, ensuring that data isn't corrupted during transmission. Think of it as a quality control checkpoint on a single segment of the network. It might use checksums or other error-detecting codes to verify the integrity of the data. If an error is detected, the Data Link Layer might request retransmission of the frame. This layer also handles media access control (MAC), which determines how devices share the same physical medium (e.g., Ethernet). MAC addresses, unique identifiers assigned to network interfaces, are used at this layer to identify devices on the local network.

The Network Layer

Now we move beyond a single network segment and into the world of routing. The Network Layer is responsible for getting data packets from one network to another. It's like the postal service, determining the best route for a letter to reach its destination, even if it involves multiple post offices (networks). The Internet

Protocol (IP) operates at this layer. IP addresses, those unique identifiers for devices on the internet, are used here. The Network Layer uses routing tables and routing protocols (like OSPF or BGP) to determine the optimal path for a packet to travel across multiple networks to reach its destination IP address. This is where the concept of internetworking comes into play, connecting different networks together.

The Transport Layer

This layer ensures reliable end-to-end communication between applications. It takes the data from the Application Layer and breaks it down into smaller segments (if necessary), adds headers containing sequence numbers and other control information, and passes them down to the Network Layer. On the receiving end, it reassembles the segments back into the original data, ensuring that they arrive in the correct order and without errors. Think of it as the delivery service that guarantees your package arrives intact and on time. Two key protocols operate at this layer: TCP (Transmission Control Protocol) and UDP (User Datagram Protocol). TCP provides a reliable, connection-oriented service, guaranteeing delivery, order, and error-free transmission. It's used for applications that require high reliability, like web browsing and file transfer. UDP, on the other hand, is a connectionless protocol that's faster but doesn't guarantee delivery or order. It's used for applications where speed is more important than reliability, like video streaming and online gaming.

The Session Layer

This layer manages the *sessions* between applications. A session is like a conversation between two programs. The Session Layer handles things like establishing, maintaining, and terminating these sessions. It's like setting up a phone call, keeping the connection active, and then hanging up when the conversation is finished. While important in the OSI model, the Session Layer is often less emphasized in practice, as its functionality is often handled by the Transport Layer or the Application Layer.

The Presentation Layer

This layer deals with data formatting and representation. It ensures that data is presented in a way that both the sender and receiver understand, even if they use different systems. Think of it as a translator, making sure everyone speaks the same "language" when it comes to data representation. It handles things like data encryption and decryption, and data compression. For example, if you're sending an image, the Presentation Layer might handle the encoding of the image data into a standard format like JPEG or PNG.

The Application Layer

This is the layer closest to the user, providing network services to applications. It's where you'll find protocols like HTTP (for web browsing), SMTP (for email), and FTP (for file transfer). This is the layer your Go network applications will often interact with. When you write a Go program that makes an HTTP request, it's interacting with the Application Layer. This layer provides the interface for applications to access the network. It's the layer where the user-facing part of network communication takes place.

While the OSI model is a valuable conceptual tool, it's important to remember that it's a *model*. Real-world network implementations often don't adhere strictly to the seven-layer structure. The TCP/IP model, which we'll discuss later, is a more practical model that's closer to how the internet actually works. However, understanding the OSI model provides a solid foundation for understanding networking principles and how the different components of a network interact.

1.2 TCP/IP Protocol Suite

Now that we've explored the OSI model, let's turn our attention to the TCP/IP protocol suite, the actual foundation of the internet. While the OSI model provides a helpful conceptual framework, the TCP/IP model is the one that's implemented in the real world. It's a more concise model, with four layers instead of seven, and it reflects the actual architecture of the internet.

The TCP/IP model is named after its two core protocols: TCP (Transmission Control Protocol) and IP (Internet Protocol). These protocols are the workhorses of internet communication, enabling data to flow reliably and efficiently across networks. Understanding the TCP/IP model is essential for anyone working with network programming, as it provides the framework for how data is transmitted and received over the internet.

Let's break down the four layers of the TCP/IP model

The Link Layer

This layer is the foundation of the TCP/IP stack, and it's responsible for the physical transmission of data over a specific network medium. It encompasses the functions of both the Physical and Data Link layers in the OSI model. This layer deals with the hardware aspects of networking, including network interface cards (NICs), cables, and physical signaling. It defines how data is encoded into electrical, optical, or radio signals and how those signals are transmitted over the physical medium. The Link Layer also handles error detection and correction on the local network, ensuring that data is transmitted reliably between directly connected devices. Examples of technologies operating at this layer include Ethernet, Wi-Fi, and Bluetooth.

The Internet Layer

This layer is the heart of the TCP/IP model, responsible for addressing and routing data packets across networks. It's the equivalent of the Network Layer in the OSI model. The Internet Protocol (IP) is the primary protocol at this layer. IP provides a mechanism for assigning unique addresses (IP addresses) to devices on the network and for routing packets based on those addresses. Think of IP addresses as the "street addresses" of the internet, allowing data to be delivered to the correct destination. The Internet Layer also handles fragmentation and reassembly of packets. If a packet is too large to be transmitted over a particular network link, it's fragmented into smaller pieces at the source and reassembled at the destination. Routing protocols, like OSPF and BGP, operate at this layer to exchange routing information between routers, enabling packets to traverse multiple networks to reach their destination.

The Transport Layer

This layer provides end-to-end communication between applications running on different hosts. It's similar to the Transport Layer in the OSI model. The two primary protocols at this layer are TCP and UDP. TCP provides a reliable, connection-oriented service. It guarantees that data is delivered in order, without errors, and without loss. It achieves this through mechanisms like acknowledgments, retransmissions, and flow control. TCP is used for applications that require high reliability, such as web browsing, email, and file transfer. UDP, on the other hand, is a connectionless protocol that doesn't provide any guarantees of delivery, order, or error-free transmission. It's faster and more efficient than TCP, but it's less reliable. UDP is used for applications where speed is more important than reliability, such as video streaming, online gaming, and DNS lookups.

The Application Layer

This is the topmost layer of the TCP/IP model, and it's where applications interact with the network. It combines the functionality of the Session, Presentation, and Application layers in the OSI model.

This layer provides a wide range of services to applications, including

- HTTP (Hypertext Transfer Protocol): Used for web browsing and accessing web resources.
- SMTP (Simple Mail Transfer Protocol): Used for sending email.
- FTP (File Transfer Protocol): Used for transferring files between computers.
- DNS (Domain Name System): Used to translate domain names (like "google.com") into IP addresses.
- Telnet: Used for remote terminal access.
- SSH (Secure Shell): Used for secure remote access and file transfer.

The Application Layer provides a standardized way for applications to access network services and exchange data, regardless of the underlying network infrastructure.

The TCP/IP model is a robust and flexible framework that has enabled the explosive growth of the internet. Its layered structure allows for modularity and interoperability, making it possible for different technologies and networks to work together seamlessly. As you delve deeper into network programming with Go, you'll gain a greater appreciation for the elegance and power of the TCP/IP protocol suite.

1.3 Sockets and Ports

In the world of networking, when applications need to communicate with each other, they don't just shout into the void. They need a structured way to connect and exchange data. This is where sockets and ports come into play. Think of them as the essential building blocks for establishing communication channels between applications, whether they're on the same computer or located across the globe.

Sockets

A socket is like a doorway to an application running on a computer. It's the endpoint of a network connection, a point where data can flow in and out. Just like a physical doorway has an address, a socket also has an address, but it's a bit more complex than your typical street address.

A socket's address consists of two parts

- IP Address: This identifies the computer on the network. It's like the street address of the building where the application resides.
- Port Number: This identifies the specific application on that computer. It's like the apartment number within the building, specifying which application should receive the data.

So, a socket address is a combination of an IP address and a port number, uniquely identifying an application on a network. When an application wants to communicate over the network, it creates a socket and binds it to a specific port. Other applications can then connect to that socket using the socket address to exchange data.

Ports

A port is a numbered communication endpoint on a computer. It's like a designated entry point for a specific application. Think of it as the apartment number within a building. Each application running on a computer is assigned a unique port number, allowing it to receive data addressed specifically to it.

Port numbers range from 0 to 65535. Some port numbers are well-known and reserved for specific services.

For example

- Port 80: Typically used for HTTP web traffic.
- Port 443: Typically used for HTTPS secure web traffic.
- Port 25: Used for SMTP email traffic.
- Port 22: Used for SSH secure remote connections.

When an application wants to listen for incoming connections, it binds a socket to a specific port. This tells the operating system that any incoming data addressed to that port should be delivered to that application.

Types of sockets

There are two main types of sockets, each suited for different types of communication

- TCP Sockets (Transmission Control Protocol): These sockets provide reliable, connection-oriented communication. They guarantee that data is delivered in order, without errors, and without loss. TCP sockets are like a dedicated phone line between two applications, ensuring a continuous and reliable connection. They are used for applications that require high reliability, such as web browsing, file transfer, and email.

- UDP Sockets (User Datagram Protocol): These sockets provide connectionless, unreliable communication. They don't guarantee delivery, order, or error-free transmission. UDP sockets are like sending a letter – you send it and hope it arrives, but there's no guarantee. They are used for applications where speed is more important than reliability, such as video streaming, online gaming, and DNS lookups.

Sockets in action

Let's say you're browsing the web. Your web browser creates a TCP socket and connects to the web server's socket, which is typically listening on port 80 (HTTP) or 443 (HTTPS). The browser sends an HTTP request over the socket to the server, requesting a specific web page. The server receives the request, processes it, and sends back the requested web page over the same socket. Your browser receives the data and renders the web page. All this communication happens through sockets, providing the essential channels for data exchange.

Go and sockets

Go provides excellent support for working with sockets through its net package. You can use this package to create sockets, establish connections, send and receive data, and handle various network operations. We'll explore the specifics of using Go's net package in later chapters.

Understanding sockets and ports is fundamental to network programming. They are the essential building blocks for establishing communication channels between applications, enabling them to exchange data and collaborate across networks. As you progress through this book, you'll gain a deeper understanding of how sockets and ports work and how to use them effectively in your Go network applications.

1.4 Network Topologies

When we talk about networks, we often focus on the individual devices and how they communicate. But just as important is the overall structure of the network – how these devices are interconnected. This is where network topologies come into play. A network topology is essentially a map, a visual representation of how devices are arranged and connected within a network. It dictates how data flows between these devices, influencing the network's performance, reliability, and security.

Understanding network topologies is crucial for designing and managing networks effectively. Different topologies have different strengths and weaknesses, and choosing the right topology for a particular network depends on factors like the size of the network, the type of applications being used, and the budget available.

Let's explore some of the most common network topologies

Bus Topology

In a bus topology, all devices are connected to a single cable, often referred to as the "bus" or "backbone." Data transmitted by any device travels along this cable in both directions, and each device checks the destination address of the data to see if it's intended for them. This topology is simple and inexpensive to implement, making it suitable for small networks. However, it has some significant drawbacks. If the main cable fails, the entire network goes down. Also, as more devices are added to the bus, performance can degrade due to increased collisions and contention for the shared cable. Bus topologies were more common in early Ethernet networks but are less prevalent today.

Star Topology

The star topology is one of the most popular network topologies today. In this topology, all devices are connected to a central device, such as a hub or switch. This central device acts as a traffic controller, receiving data from one device and forwarding it to the intended recipient. The star topology offers several advantages over the bus topology. It's more reliable because a failure in one cable or device doesn't affect the rest of the network. It also offers better performance, as each device has a dedicated connection to the central hub or switch, reducing collisions and contention. Star topologies are commonly used in Ethernet networks and Wi-Fi networks.

Ring Topology

In a ring topology, devices are connected in a closed loop or ring. Data travels around the ring in one direction, and each device acts as a repeater, receiving data and retransmitting it to the next device in the ring. This topology can be efficient for small networks, as data travels in a predictable path. However, it has some disadvantages. If one device fails, the entire ring can be disrupted. Also, adding or removing devices can be complex, as it requires breaking the ring. Ring topologies were used in some early token ring networks but are less common today.

Mesh Topology

A mesh topology provides high redundancy and fault tolerance by interconnecting devices with multiple paths. In a full mesh topology, every device is connected to every other device. This provides multiple routes for data to travel, so if one link fails, data can be rerouted through another path. Mesh topologies are very reliable but can be expensive to implement, as they require a large number of connections. Partial mesh topologies, where only some devices are interconnected with multiple paths, are more common. Mesh topologies are often used in critical applications where high availability is essential, such as telecommunications networks and industrial control systems.

Tree Topology

A tree topology is a hierarchical structure that combines elements of other topologies, often resembling an inverted tree. It has a root node at the top, and branches of nodes extending downwards. This topology is well-suited for large networks with multiple levels of hierarchy, such as corporate networks. It allows for efficient management and organization of devices. However, it can be susceptible to single points of failure at higher levels of the hierarchy.

Choosing the right topology

The choice of network topology depends on a variety of factors, including

- Network size: Small networks may be well-served by simple topologies like bus or star, while larger networks may require more complex topologies like mesh or tree.
- Cost: The cost of cabling and network devices can vary significantly depending on the topology.
- Reliability: Some topologies offer higher redundancy and fault tolerance than others.
- Performance: The topology can affect network performance, particularly in terms of bandwidth and latency.
- Security: The topology can influence the security of the network, as some topologies may be more vulnerable to certain types of attacks.

Network topologies are a fundamental aspect of network design and management. Understanding the different topologies and their characteristics is essential for building and maintaining efficient, reliable, and secure networks. As you gain more experience with network programming, you'll develop a deeper appreciation for how the choice of topology can impact the overall performance and functionality of a network.

1.5 Why Go for Network Programming?

Now, you might be wondering, "Why Go? There are so many programming languages out there. What makes Go particularly well-suited for network programming?" That's a great question, and the answer lies in a combination of factors that make Go a powerful and efficient choice for building network applications.

Concurrency Made Easy

One of Go's standout features is its built-in support for concurrency. Concurrency means the ability to execute multiple tasks seemingly at the same time. In network programming, this is essential for handling multiple client connections simultaneously without blocking or slowing down the application. Go achieves concurrency through *goroutines* and *channels*.

Goroutines are lightweight, independently executing functions. Think of them as mini-programs running within your main program. Creating a goroutine is as simple as adding the go keyword before a function call. This allows you to handle each client connection in its own goroutine, ensuring that one slow connection doesn't hold up the entire application.

Channels provide a safe and efficient way for goroutines to communicate and share data. They're like synchronized pipes that allow data to flow between goroutines without the risk of race conditions or data corruption. This makes it easy to coordinate and manage concurrent operations in your network applications.

Performance that Matters

Network applications often need to handle a high volume of requests and data, so performance is critical. Go excels in this area. It's a compiled language, meaning the code is translated directly into machine code that can be executed efficiently by the processor. This results in fast execution speeds and efficient resource utilization.

Furthermore, Go's runtime environment is designed for performance. It includes a highly optimized garbage collector that manages memory automatically, minimizing pauses and ensuring smooth operation. This combination of compiled code and efficient runtime makes Go a top contender for building high-performance network applications.

A Rich Standard Library

Go's standard library is a treasure trove of packages that simplify network programming. The net package provides a comprehensive set of tools for working with sockets, TCP, UDP, and other network protocols. You can easily create sockets, establish connections, send and receive data, and handle various network operations.

The net/http package provides everything you need to build web servers and clients. You can handle HTTP requests and responses, manage cookies, and implement various web protocols. Go's standard library also includes support for encoding and decoding data in various formats, such as JSON, XML, and Protocol Buffers, which are commonly used in network communication.

Simplicity and Readability

Go's syntax is clean, concise, and easy to read. This makes it easier to write and maintain network code, especially in complex projects. The language emphasizes clarity and simplicity, reducing the cognitive burden on developers and making it easier to reason about the code.

Cross-Platform Compatibility

Go is a cross-platform language, meaning you can compile your Go code to run on various operating systems, including Windows, macOS, Linux, and various Unix flavors. This makes it easy to deploy your network applications across different platforms without having to worry about platform-specific dependencies or code modifications.

A Thriving Ecosystem

Go has a growing and vibrant community of developers, which means there are plenty of resources, libraries, and frameworks available to help you build network applications. You can find third-party packages for various network protocols, security features, and performance optimizations. This active community ensures that Go stays up-to-date with the latest networking trends and technologies.

Real-World Examples

Go's strengths in concurrency, performance, and networking have made it a popular choice for building a wide range of network applications, including:

- Web servers and APIs: Go powers high-traffic websites and APIs, handling millions of requests concurrently. Examples include Docker, Kubernetes, and Dropbox.
- Microservices: Go's lightweight concurrency and efficient resource utilization make it ideal for building microservices architectures, where applications are broken down into small, independent services that communicate over a network.

- Networking tools: Go is used to build networking tools like network scanners, proxies, and load balancers.
- Messaging systems: Go's concurrency features are well-suited for building real-time messaging systems and chat applications.

Go's combination of concurrency, performance, a rich standard library, simplicity, and cross-platform compatibility makes it an excellent choice for network programming. Whether you're building a simple web server or a complex distributed system, Go provides the tools and features you need to create robust and efficient network applications.

Chapter 2: Working with Sockets in Go

In this chapter, we'll explore the core of network programming in Go: working with sockets. Remember those doorways we talked about in the previous chapter? Now, we'll learn how to build them, open them, send messages through them, and close them properly.

2.1 Creating TCP Sockets

Let's get down to business and start creating some TCP sockets in Go! Remember, TCP is our reliable workhorse for network communication, ensuring that data gets delivered in order and without errors. Think of it as setting up a dedicated phone line between two applications.

In Go, we use the net package to work with sockets. This package provides a powerful set of tools for creating, managing, and interacting with various types of sockets, including TCP, UDP, and Unix sockets. It's your go-to toolkit for all things socket-related in Go.

To create a TCP socket, we use the net.Listen() function. This function is like setting up a listening post, telling the operating system, "Hey, I'm ready to receive connections on this address."

It takes two arguments

- network**:** This specifies the network type, which in our case is "tcp". It tells the Listen() function that we want to create a TCP socket.
- address**:** This specifies the IP address and port number to bind the socket to. It's like giving our socket an address so other applications can find it. The address is typically specified in the format ":port", where port is the port number. For example, ":8080" would bind the socket to

port 8080 on all available network interfaces. You can also specify a specific IP address, like "127.0.0.1:8080" to bind to port 8080 on the local loopback interface.

Here's a simple example that demonstrates how to create a TCP socket and listen for incoming connections

Code snippet

```
package main


import (

  "fmt"

  "net"

)



func main() {

  // Listen on TCP port 8080 on all available
network interfaces

  listener, err:= net.Listen("tcp", ":8080")

  if err!= nil {

    fmt.Println("Error listening:", err.Error())

    return

  }
```

```go
  defer listener.Close() // Ensure the listener is
closed when the function exits


  fmt.Println("Listening on:8080...")


  // Accept incoming connections

  for {

    conn, err:= listener.Accept()

    if err!= nil {

      fmt.Println("Error accepting connection:",
err.Error())

      return

    }

    // Handle the connection (e.g., read data, send
a response)

    go handleConnection(conn) // Process the
connection concurrently

  }

}


func handleConnection(conn net.Conn) {

  defer conn.Close() // Ensure the connection is
closed when the function exits
```

```go
// Read data from the connection
buffer := make(byte, 1024)
n, err := conn.Read(buffer)
if err != nil {
  fmt.Println("Error reading:", err.Error())
  return
}


// Process the received data (e.g., print it)
fmt.Println("Received:", string(buffer[:n]))


// Send a response back to the client
response := "Hello from the server!"
_, err = conn.Write(byte(response))
if err != nil {
  fmt.Println("Error writing:", err.Error())
  return
}
}
```

In this example, we first create a TCP listener using net.Listen(). If there's an error, we print it and exit. Otherwise, we defer the closing of the listener using defer listener.Close(). This ensures that the listener is closed properly when the function exits, even if there are errors.

Next, we enter an infinite loop (for {}) to continuously accept incoming connections. The listener.Accept() function blocks until a client connects to the socket. Once a client connects, Accept() returns a net.Conn object, which represents the connection to the client. This net.Conn object is like a two-way communication channel between the server and the client.

We then call the handleConnection() function to handle the connection. We use go handleConnection(conn) to start a new goroutine for each connection. This allows the server to handle multiple connections concurrently without blocking.

The handleConnection() function takes the net.Conn object as an argument. It first defers the closing of the connection using defer conn.Close(). Then, it reads data from the connection using conn.Read(), processes the data, and sends a response back to the client using conn.Write().

This example demonstrates the basic structure of a TCP server in Go. It listens for incoming connections, accepts them, and handles each connection concurrently. In later chapters, we'll build upon this foundation to create more complex and sophisticated network applications.

2.2 Creating UDP Sockets

Now that we've explored the world of TCP sockets, let's shift our focus to UDP sockets. Remember, UDP is our speed demon, offering a connectionless and less reliable (but faster!) way to communicate over networks. Think of it as sending a postcard: you put it in the mailbox and hope it reaches its destination, but there's no guarantee.

Just like with TCP sockets, we use the net package in Go to work with UDP sockets. However, instead of establishing a connection like we do with TCP, UDP communication involves sending individual packets of data to a specific address. Each packet is like a self-contained message with its own addressing information.

To create a UDP socket, we use the net.ListenPacket() function. This function is similar to net.Listen(), but instead of creating a listener that accepts connections, it creates a socket that's ready to send and receive individual packets. It takes two arguments:

- network: This specifies the network type, which for UDP is "udp". This tells the ListenPacket() function that we want to create a UDP socket.
- address: This specifies the IP address and port number to bind the socket to. It's like giving our socket a return address so that responses can be sent back to us. The address format is the same as for TCP sockets, typically ":port" to bind to a specific port on all interfaces, or "ip:port" to bind to a specific port on a specific IP address.

Here's a simple example that demonstrates how to create a UDP socket and receive data

```
Code snippet

package main


import (

  "fmt"
```

```go
    "net"

)


func main() {

  // Listen on UDP port 9090 on all available
network interfaces

  conn, err:= net.ListenPacket("udp", ":9090")

  if err!= nil {

   fmt.Println("Error listening:", err.Error())

    return

  }

  defer conn.Close() // Ensure the connection is
closed when the function exits


  fmt.Println("Listening on:9090...")


  // Receive data

  for {

   buffer:= make(byte, 1024)

   n, addr, err:= conn.ReadFrom(buffer)

   if err!= nil {
```

```go
        fmt.Println("Error reading:", err.Error())

        return

    }


    // Process the received data (e.g., print it)

    fmt.Println("Received:", string(buffer[:n]),
"from", addr)


    // Send a response back to the client

    response:= "Hello from the server!"

    _, err = conn.WriteTo(byte(response), addr)

    if err!= nil {

      fmt.Println("Error writing:", err.Error())

      return

    }

  }

}
```

In this example, we first create a UDP socket using net.ListenPacket(). If there's an error, we print it and exit. Otherwise, we defer the closing of the socket using defer conn.Close(). This ensures that the socket is closed properly when the function exits, even if there are errors.

Next, we enter an infinite loop (for {}) to continuously receive data.

The conn.ReadFrom() function reads data from the socket and returns three values

- n: The number of bytes read.
- addr: The address of the sender.
- err: An error, if any.

We then process the received data (in this case, we simply print it along with the sender's address) and send a response back to the sender using conn.WriteTo().

This function takes two arguments

- b: The data to send, as a byte slice.
- addr: The address to send the data to.

This example demonstrates the basic structure of a UDP server in Go. It listens for incoming packets, receives them, and sends responses back to the senders. It's important to note that UDP communication is connectionless, so there's no guarantee that the response will reach the sender, or that the sender will be listening for a response.

UDP sockets are commonly used in applications where speed and efficiency are more important than reliability, such as

- Streaming media: Video and audio streaming often use UDP because occasional packet loss is less noticeable than the delays that TCP might introduce.

- Online gaming: Fast response times are crucial in online games, and UDP's lower overhead can provide a better gaming experience.
- DNS lookups: DNS queries and responses typically use UDP because they are small and require quick turnaround times.

Go's net package provides a straightforward way to work with UDP sockets, allowing you to build applications that leverage the speed and efficiency of UDP communication. As you progress through this book, you'll explore more advanced techniques for using UDP sockets, including techniques for improving reliability and handling multicast communication.

2.3 Establishing Connections

We've learned how to create TCP and UDP sockets, which is like building the doorways for communication. But with TCP, before any data can flow, we need to establish a proper connection—like dialing a phone number to reach the other party. UDP, being connectionless, doesn't require this step. Let's focus on how TCP connections are established in Go.

Remember the net.Listen() function we used to create a TCP socket? That sets up the server to listen for incoming connection requests. It's like waiting by the phone, ready to answer when someone calls. The Accept() method on the listener then plays the role of picking up the phone and establishing that connection.

On the client-side, we use the net.Dial() function. This is analogous to dialing the phone number. It initiates the connection request to the server's listening socket.

Dial() takes two arguments

- network: This specifies the network type, which, as you know, is "tcp" for TCP connections.

- **address:** This is the server's address, including the IP address and port number. It's like the phone number you're dialing to reach the server.

Here's a simple example of a TCP client establishing a connection to a server

Code snippet

```
package main

import (

    "fmt"

    "net"

)


func main() {

    // Connect to the server on TCP port 8080

    conn, err := net.Dial("tcp", "localhost:8080")

    if err != nil {

        fmt.Println("Error dialing:",
err.Error())

        return

    }
```

```go
    defer conn.Close() // Ensure the connection
is closed when done


    // Send data to the server

    message := "Hello from the client!"

    _, err = conn.Write(byte(message))

    if err != nil {

        fmt.Println("Error writing:",
err.Error())

        return

    }


    // Receive a response from the server

    buffer := make(byte, 1024)

    n, err := conn.Read(buffer)

    if err != nil {

        fmt.Println("Error reading:",
err.Error())

        return

    }


    // Print the received response
```

```
fmt.Println("Received:", string(buffer[:n]))
```

}

In this example, net.Dial() attempts to connect to the server running on localhost:8080. If the connection is successful, it returns a net.Conn object, which represents the established connection. This object is then used for sending and receiving data. If there's an error during the connection attempt, it's important to handle it gracefully, as shown in the example.

The TCP Handshake

Under the hood, TCP uses a three-way handshake to establish a connection.

It's like a short conversation that goes like this

1. Client: "Hello, Server! Are you there? I'd like to talk. (SYN)"
2. Server: "Yes, Client, I hear you! I'm ready to chat. (SYN-ACK)"
3. Client: "Great, let's talk! (ACK)"

This handshake ensures that both the client and server are ready to communicate before any data is exchanged. It synchronizes their state and establishes a reliable connection.

Error Handling

When establishing connections, things can go wrong. The server might be down, the network might be unreachable, or the port might be blocked. It's crucial to handle these potential errors gracefully. In the example above, we check for errors returned by net.Dial() and print an error message if something goes wrong. In real-world applications, you might want to implement more sophisticated error handling, such as retrying the connection attempt or providing informative feedback to the user.

Connection Lifecycle

Once a TCP connection is established, it remains active until it's explicitly closed by either the client or the server. This allows for continuous, bidirectional communication. It's like having a phone conversation where you can talk back and forth until one of you hangs up. We'll discuss how to close connections properly in a later section.

Understanding how to establish TCP connections is fundamental to network programming in Go. It allows you to create client applications that can connect to servers and exchange data reliably. As you progress through this book, you'll build upon this knowledge to create more complex and sophisticated network applications.

2.4 Sending and Receiving Data

Alright, we've built our communication channels using sockets and even established connections for our reliable TCP conversations. Now comes the exciting part: actually sending and receiving data through these channels! This is where the real magic of network programming happens, enabling applications to exchange information and collaborate across networks.

In Go, the net.Conn object, which represents our connection, provides the tools we need for this data exchange. It's like having a two-way pipe where we can write data to send it out and read data to receive incoming information.

Sending Data with Write()

To send data through a connection, we use the Write() method of the net.Conn object. This method takes a byte slice (byte) as input and sends it over the network to the other end of the connection. Think of it as writing a message on a piece of paper and sending it through the pipe.

Here's a simple example

```
Code snippet

//... (assuming conn is a net.Conn object)


message:= "Hello from the other side!"

_, err:= conn.Write(byte(message))

if err!= nil {

    fmt.Println("Error writing:", err.Error())

    return

}
```

In this example, we convert the string "Hello from the other side!" into a byte slice and send it through the connection using conn.Write(). The Write() method returns the number of bytes written and an error, if any. It's always a good practice to check for errors to ensure that the data was sent successfully.

Receiving Data with Read()

To receive data from a connection, we use the Read() method of the net.Conn object. This method takes a byte slice as input and fills it with the received data. It's like holding a container under the pipe and waiting for data to fill it up.

Here's an example

```
Code snippet

//... (assuming conn is a net.Conn object)
```

```
buffer := make(byte, 1024) // Create a buffer to
store the received data

n, err := conn.Read(buffer)

if err != nil {

    fmt.Println("Error reading:", err.Error())

    return

}



// Process the received data

fmt.Println("Received:", string(buffer[:n]))
```

In this example, we create a buffer of 1024 bytes to store the received data. The Read() method reads data from the connection and fills the buffer. It returns the number of bytes read (n) and an error, if any. We then process the received data, which in this case is simply printing it to the console.

Important Considerations

- Buffer Size: When receiving data, it's important to choose an appropriate buffer size. If the buffer is too small, you might not be able to receive the entire message at once. If it's too large, you might waste memory.
- Error Handling: Always check for errors returned by Write() and Read(). Network communication is inherently prone to errors, and it's crucial to handle them gracefully to prevent your application from crashing.

- Data Formats: When exchanging data, you need to agree on a data format with the other end of the connection. This could be a simple string, a structured format like JSON or XML, or a custom binary format.
- TCP vs. UDP: The way you send and receive data might differ slightly depending on whether you're using TCP or UDP sockets. With TCP, you have a continuous, reliable connection, so you can send and receive data in a stream-like fashion. With UDP, you send and receive individual packets, so you need to handle addressing and potential packet loss.

Real-World Examples

Sending and receive data is the core of many network applications.

Here are a couple of examples

- Chat Applications: When you send a message in a chat application, your message is encoded into a specific format (e.g., JSON) and sent over a TCP socket to the server. The server then relays the message to the recipient's socket.
- File Transfer: When you download a file from the internet, your web browser establishes a TCP connection to the web server and requests the file. The server sends the file data over the connection, and your browser receives and saves it to your computer.

By mastering the techniques of sending and receiving data with Go sockets, you gain the ability to build a wide range of network applications, from simple chat programs to complex distributed systems. So, go ahead and experiment with these concepts, and see what you can create!

2.5 Handling Disconnections

In the world of network programming, connections are like conversations: they have a beginning and an end. Just as it's important to establish connections gracefully, it's equally important to handle disconnections properly. When a connection is closed abruptly or unexpectedly, it can lead to resource leaks, data corruption, and even application crashes. Therefore, understanding how to handle disconnections is crucial for building robust and reliable network applications.

In Go, we use the Close() method of the net.Conn object to close a connection. This method sends a signal to the other end of the connection, indicating that the connection is being closed. It's like saying "goodbye" at the end of a phone call.

Graceful Disconnections

A graceful disconnection involves properly closing the connection from both ends. This ensures that any pending data is transmitted and that both sides are aware that the connection is ending.

Here's how you typically handle a graceful disconnection

- Client-side: When the client is done sending data, it sends a "close" signal to the server. The server, upon receiving this signal, acknowledges the close request and closes its end of the connection. The client then receives the acknowledgment and closes its end of the connection.
- Server-side: The server can also initiate a graceful disconnection by sending a "close" signal to the client. The client acknowledges the request and closes its end of the connection, and the server then closes its end.

This coordinated closure ensures that both sides have a chance to clean up any resources and prevent data loss.

Unexpected Disconnections

Unfortunately, not all disconnections are graceful.

Network connections can be interrupted due to various reasons, such as

- Network errors: The network connection might drop due to a network outage, a router failure, or other network problems.
- Application crashes: One of the applications involved in the connection might crash or terminate unexpectedly.
- Forced closures: A user might forcibly close the connection, or a firewall might terminate the connection.

When these unexpected disconnections occur, it's important to handle them gracefully to prevent your application from crashing or behaving erratically. Go provides mechanisms to detect and handle these situations.

Detecting Disconnections

You can detect a disconnection by checking for errors returned by the Read() or Write() methods. If a connection is closed, these methods will typically return an error indicating that the connection is closed or reset.

Handling Disconnections

When a disconnection is detected, you should take appropriate actions, such as

- Closing the connection: If the connection is still open, close it using the Close() method.
- Cleaning up resources: Release any resources associated with the connection, such as memory buffers or file handles.

- Notifying the user: If the disconnection affects the user experience, provide informative feedback to the user, such as a "connection lost" message.
- Reconnecting (optional): If the application requires a persistent connection, you might attempt to reconnect to the server.

Using defer for Automatic Closure

Go provides a convenient mechanism called defer to ensure that connections are closed properly, even in the event of errors or unexpected exits. The defer statement schedules a function call to be executed when the surrounding function exits. This is particularly useful for closing connections, as it guarantees that the Close() method will be called even if there are errors or panics within the function.

Here's an example

Code snippet

```
conn, err:= net.Dial("tcp", "localhost:8080")

if err!= nil {

    // Handle error

}

defer conn.Close() // This ensures that
conn.Close() is called when the function exits


//... use the connection...
```

Real-World Examples

Handling disconnections is a crucial aspect of many network applications

- Web Servers: When a user closes their web browser, the web server needs to detect the disconnection and close the corresponding connection to free up resources.
- Chat Applications: If a user disconnects from a chat room, the server needs to handle the disconnection gracefully, removing the user from the chat room and notifying other users.
- Online Games: If a player disconnects from an online game, the server needs to handle the disconnection, potentially removing the player from the game or pausing their progress.

By mastering the techniques for handling disconnections in Go, you can build robust and reliable network applications that can gracefully handle unexpected events and provide a smooth user experience.

2.6 Working with Non-blocking Sockets

Up until now, we've been working with blocking sockets. This means that when you call a function like Read() or Write() on a socket, the function doesn't return until the operation is complete. In other words, your program execution halts, waiting for the network operation to finish. This can be fine for simple applications, but it becomes a bottleneck when you need to handle multiple connections simultaneously or perform other tasks while waiting for network events.

Think of it like waiting in a long line at the post office. If you're the only one there, it's not a big deal. But if there are many people behind you, and you're waiting for a package that might take a while to arrive, it becomes inefficient. You're blocking everyone else behind you.

Non-blocking sockets, on the other hand, allow you to check the status of a socket operation without blocking. It's like asking the postal worker, "Is my package here yet?" If it is, you can take it and go. If not, you can come back later or do other things while you wait.

How Non-blocking Sockets Work

When you set a socket to non-blocking mode, the Read() and Write() functions will return immediately, even if the operation is not complete. They will typically return an error indicating that the operation would block ("would block" error). This allows you to check the status of the socket without getting stuck.

Setting Sockets to Non-blocking Mode

In Go, you can set a socket to non-blocking mode using the SetNonblock() method of the net.Conn object.

Here's an example

```
Code snippet

conn, err:= net.Dial("tcp", "localhost:8080")

if err!= nil {

    // Handle error

}


err = conn.SetNonblock(true)
```

```
if err!= nil {

    // Handle error

}
```

```
// Now conn is a non-blocking socket
```

Techniques for Working with Non-blocking Sockets

There are a few common techniques for working with non-blocking sockets in Go

- Polling: You can periodically check the status of the socket using Read() or Write(). If the operation is complete, the function will return the data or the number of bytes written. If not, it will return a "would block" error. This approach is simple but can be inefficient if you're polling too frequently.
- Setting Deadlines: You can set a deadline on the socket using the SetDeadline(), SetReadDeadline(), or SetWriteDeadline() methods. This tells the socket to time out if the operation doesn't complete within the specified time. This can prevent your program from getting stuck indefinitely waiting for a slow or unresponsive connection.
- Using select with Channels: This is a more advanced technique that involves using channels and the select statement to monitor multiple sockets simultaneously. You can create a channel for each socket and use select to wait for events on any of the channels. This allows you to handle events from multiple sockets concurrently without blocking on any single socket.

Example with Deadlines

Code snippet

```
conn, err:= net.Dial("tcp", "localhost:8080")

if err!= nil {

    // Handle error

}

defer conn.Close()


conn.SetReadDeadline(time.Now().Add(1 *
time.Second)) // Set a 1-second read deadline


buffer:= make(byte, 1024)

n, err:= conn.Read(buffer)

if err!= nil {

    if neterr, ok:= err.(net.Error); ok &&
neterr.Timeout() {

        fmt.Println("Read timeout")

    } else {

        fmt.Println("Error reading:",
err.Error())

    }

    return
```

```
}
```

```
fmt.Println("Received:", string(buffer[:n]))
```

In this example, we set a 1-second read deadline on the socket. If no data is received within 1 second, the Read() function will return a timeout error.

Real-World Examples

Non-blocking sockets are essential for building high-performance network applications that need to handle multiple connections concurrently or perform other tasks while waiting for network events.

Here are some examples

- Web Servers: A web server needs to handle many client requests simultaneously. Non-blocking sockets allow the server to process requests concurrently without blocking on any single request.
- Chat Applications: A chat server needs to monitor multiple client connections for incoming messages. Non-blocking sockets allow the server to efficiently check for new messages without blocking on any particular client.
- Real-time Applications: Applications that require real-time interaction, such as online games or collaborative tools, often use non-blocking sockets to ensure responsiveness and low latency.

By understanding and utilizing non-blocking sockets, you can significantly enhance the performance and responsiveness of your Go network applications.

Chapter 3: Handling Network Protocols

In this chapter, we'll focus on some of the most common protocols you'll encounter in network programming: HTTP, SMTP, and POP3. We'll also touch upon how to implement your own custom protocols when the need arises.

3.1 HTTP Protocol

Let's talk about HTTP, the protocol that powers the web. It's the unsung hero behind every web page you visit, every image you see, and every video you stream. HTTP, or Hypertext Transfer Protocol, is the language that web browsers and web servers use to communicate with each other. It's a set of rules that govern how clients request resources and how servers respond to those requests.

Think of HTTP as a conversation between a customer (the web browser) and a waiter (the web server) at a restaurant. The customer makes requests ("Can I have the menu? I'll take the spaghetti and meatballs."), and the waiter responds ("Here's the menu. Your food will be right out."). HTTP defines the format of these requests and responses, ensuring that both parties understand each other.

The Request-Response Cycle

HTTP follows a simple request-response cycle. It starts with the client sending a request to the server.

This request includes

- A method: This indicates the action the client wants to perform. Common methods include GET (to retrieve data), POST (to submit data), PUT (to update data), and DELETE (to delete data).
- A URL: This specifies the resource the client is requesting. It's like telling the waiter what dish you want to order.
- Headers: These provide additional information about the request, such as the client's preferred language or the types of content it can accept.
- A body (optional): This contains data that the client is sending to the server, such as form data or JSON payload.

The server receives the request, processes it, and sends back a response.

The response includes

- A status code: This indicates whether the request was successful. For example, a 200 OK status code means the request was successful, while a 404 Not Found status code means the requested resource was not found.
- Headers: These provide additional information about the response, such as the content type or any cookies being set.
- A body (optional): This contains the data that the server is sending back to the client, such as the requested web page or the result of a database query.

HTTP in Go

Go's standard library provides excellent support for HTTP through the net/http package. This package provides functions for creating web servers, making HTTP requests, and handling various aspects of HTTP communication.

Creating a Web Server

Here's a slightly more elaborate example of creating a web server in Go

Code snippet

```
package main


import (

  "fmt"

  "net/http"

)



func helloHandler(w http.ResponseWriter, r
*http.Request) {

  fmt.Fprintf(w, "Hello, you've requested: %s\n",
r.URL.Path)

}



func main() {

  http.HandleFunc("/", helloHandler) // Handle
requests to the root path
```

```go
http.HandleFunc("/about", func(w
http.ResponseWriter, r *http.Request) {

  fmt.Fprintln(w, "This is the about page.")

}) // Handle requests to /about


  fmt.Println("Starting server on:8080...")

  err:= http.ListenAndServe(":8080", nil)

  if err!= nil {

    fmt.Println("Error starting server:",
err.Error())

  }

}
```

In this example, we define two handler functions: one for the root path ("/") and one for the "/about" path. Each handler function writes a different response to the client.

Making HTTP Requests

To make an HTTP request in Go, you can use functions like http.Get(), http.Post(), http.Put(), and http.Delete(). These functions correspond to the different HTTP methods.

Here's an example of making a POST request

```
Code snippet

package main
```

```go
import (

  "bytes"

  "fmt"

  "io"

  "net/http"

)


func main() {

  jsonStr:=byte(`{"title":"Buy cheese and bread
for breakfast."}`)

  req, err:= http.NewRequest("POST",
"https://www.example.com/todos",
bytes.NewBuffer(jsonStr))

  if err!= nil {

    fmt.Println("Error creating request:",
err.Error())

    return

  }

  req.Header.Set("Content-Type",
"application/json")


  client:= &http.Client{}

  resp, err:= client.Do(req)
```

```go
if err!= nil {

  fmt.Println("Error making request:",
err.Error())

  return

}

defer resp.Body.Close()


fmt.Println("response Status:", resp.Status)

fmt.Println("response Headers:", resp.Header)

body, _:= io.ReadAll(resp.Body)

fmt.Println("response Body:", string(body))

}
```

In this example, we create a POST request with a JSON payload and send it to the server. We then print the response status, headers, and body.

Beyond the Basics

The net/http package provides a rich set of features for working with HTTP, including

- Handling different HTTP methods: You can handle various HTTP methods, such as GET, POST, PUT, DELETE, and others, allowing you to build RESTful APIs and handle different types of client requests.
- Setting headers and cookies: You can set custom headers in requests and responses, and you can manage cookies to store information about the client's session.

- Handling file uploads and downloads: You can handle file uploads from clients and serve files for download.
- Implementing authentication and authorization: You can implement various authentication and authorization mechanisms to protect your web applications.
- Creating websockets: You can use the golang.org/x/net/websocket package to create WebSocket connections for real-time, bidirectional communication.

HTTP is a fundamental protocol for network programming, and Go's net/http package provides a powerful and flexible toolkit for working with it. Whether you're building web servers, making HTTP requests, or creating complex web applications, Go has you covered.

3.2 SMTP Protocol

Email remains one of the most fundamental forms of communication on the internet. Whether it's for personal messages, business correspondence, or automated notifications, sending emails programmatically is a common task for many applications. This is where SMTP comes in.

SMTP, or Simple Mail Transfer Protocol, is the protocol that defines how email servers communicate with each other to deliver emails. It's like the postal service of the internet, with a set of rules for how messages are addressed, formatted, and delivered.

How SMTP Works

When you send an email, your email client (e.g., Outlook, Gmail) doesn't directly deliver the email to the recipient's inbox. Instead, it connects to an SMTP server and hands off the email to the server. The SMTP server then acts like a relay, forwarding the email to other SMTP servers until it reaches the recipient's mail server. The recipient's mail server then delivers the email to their inbox.

SMTP in Go

Go's standard library provides the net/smtp package, which offers functions for sending emails over SMTP. This package makes it straightforward to integrate email sending capabilities into your Go applications.

Sending an Email with Go

Here's a breakdown of how to send an email using Go

```
Code snippet

package main


import (

  "fmt"

  "net/smtp"

)


func main() {

  // Sender data.

  from:= "sender@example.com"

  password:= "password123" // Replace with your
actual password
```

```go
// Receiver email address.

to:=string{

  "recipient@example.net",

}


// Email subject and body.

subject:= "Subject: Greetings from Go!\n"

body:= "This is an email from a Go program.\n"

message:=byte(subject + body)


// Connect to the SMTP server.

auth:= smtp.PlainAuth("", from, password,
"smtp.example.com") // Replace with your SMTP
server

err:= smtp.SendMail("smtp.example.com:587",
auth, from, to, message) // Replace with your
SMTP server and port

if err!= nil {

  fmt.Println("Error sending email:",
err.Error())

  return

}
```

```
fmt.Println("Email sent successfully!")

}
```

In this example

1. We define the sender's email address (from) and password (password).
2. We specify the recipient's email address (to).
3. We construct the email message, including the subject and body.
4. We use smtp.PlainAuth() to authenticate with the SMTP server. This function takes the sender's email, password, and the SMTP server's address as arguments.
5. We use smtp.SendMail() to send the email. This function takes the SMTP server's address, authentication information, sender's address, recipient's address, and the email message as arguments.

Important Considerations

- Authentication: Most SMTP servers require authentication to prevent spam and unauthorized access. The smtp.PlainAuth() function provides a simple way to authenticate with the server using a username and password. Other authentication mechanisms, such as OAuth2, might be required for some servers.
- TLS/SSL: For secure email transmission, you should use TLS/SSL encryption. The smtp.SendMail() function typically uses TLS by default if the server supports it. You can also explicitly enable TLS using the smtp.DialTLS() function.
- Error Handling: As with any network operation, it's important to handle potential errors during email sending. The smtp.SendMail() function returns an error if there's a

problem, and you should handle this error gracefully in your application.

- Email Formatting: Ensure that your email messages are properly formatted according to RFC 5322, the standard for internet email messages. This includes using the correct headers and formatting the message body appropriately.

Real-World Examples

Sending emails programmatically has numerous applications

- Automated Notifications: Sending notifications to users about account activity, order updates, or system alerts.
- Newsletters and Marketing Emails: Sending bulk emails to subscribers or customers.
- Password Resets: Sending password reset emails to users who have forgotten their passwords.
- Contact Forms: Processing contact forms and sending the submitted information to the website owner.

Go's net/smtp package provides a straightforward way to integrate email sending capabilities into your Go applications, enabling you to automate communication and enhance user experience.

3.3 POP3 Protocol

While SMTP handles the sending of emails, POP3 (Post Office Protocol version 3) takes care of the receiving end. It's the protocol that allows you to retrieve emails from a mail server and download them to your local machine. Think of it as going to your mailbox and collecting your letters. POP3 allows your email client to access your mailbox on the server and fetch the messages waiting for you.

How POP3 Works

When you use an email client that supports POP3 (like Thunderbird or Outlook), it connects to the POP3 server and authenticates using your username and password. It then retrieves the emails from your mailbox on the server and typically deletes them from the server, storing them locally on your computer. This means you can access your emails even when you're offline.

POP3 in Go

Go provides the net/pop3 package in its standard library, which offers functions for interacting with POP3 servers. You can use this package to connect to a POP3 server, authenticate, retrieve emails, and manage your mailbox.

Retrieving Emails with Go

Here's an example of how to use Go to retrieve emails from a POP3 server

```
Code snippet

package main


import (

  "fmt"

  "net/pop3"

)


func main() {
```

```go
// Connect to the POP3 server.

client, err:= pop3.Dial("pop.example.com:110")
// Replace with your POP3 server and port

if err!= nil {

  fmt.Println("Error connecting to server:",
err.Error())

  return

}

defer client.Quit() // Close the connection when
done


// Authenticate.

err = client.Auth("username", "password") //
Replace with your username and password

if err!= nil {

  fmt.Println("Error authenticating:",
err.Error())

  return

}


// Get the number of messages.

count, err:= client.Stat()

if err!= nil {
```

```go
        fmt.Println("Error getting message count:",
err.Error())

        return

    }



    fmt.Println("Message count:", count)



    // Retrieve the messages.

    for i:= 1; i <= count; i++ {

        msg, err:= client.Retr(i) // Retrieve the i-th
message

        if err!= nil {

            fmt.Println("Error retrieving message:",
err.Error())

            return

        }



        fmt.Println("Message", i, ":\n", string(msg))

    }

}
```

In this example

1. We use pop3.Dial() to connect to the POP3 server. This function takes the server address and port as arguments.
2. We authenticate with the server using client.Auth(), providing the username and password.
3. We use client.Stat() to get the number of messages in the mailbox.
4. We loop through the messages and retrieve each one using client.Retr(). This function retrieves the raw email message as a byte slice.
5. We print the retrieved messages to the console.

Important Considerations

- Security: POP3 typically transmits data in plain text, including your username and password. To secure the communication, you should use POP3S, which is POP3 over SSL/TLS. This encrypts the communication and protects your credentials.
- Deleting Emails: By default, POP3 deletes emails from the server after they are retrieved. You can change this behavior by using the client.Dele() function to explicitly delete messages or by configuring your email client to keep copies of messages on the server.
- Email Parsing: The net/pop3 package retrieves raw email messages. To parse these messages and extract information like the sender, recipient, subject, and body, you can use the net/mail package, which provides functions for parsing email headers and bodies.
- Alternatives to POP3: While POP3 is a common protocol for retrieving emails, there are other protocols available, such as IMAP (Internet Message Access Protocol). IMAP offers more advanced features, such as synchronizing emails

across multiple devices and accessing emails without downloading them.

Real-World Examples

POP3 is widely used in email clients to retrieve emails from mail servers.

Here are some examples of how you might use POP3 in Go applications

- Email Monitoring: You could build an application that monitors an email inbox for specific messages, such as order confirmations or support requests.
- Email Backup: You could create a tool that backs up emails from a POP3 server to a local file or database.
- Email Filtering: You could implement an email filtering system that analyzes emails retrieved from a POP3 server and categorizes them based on their content.

By understanding and utilizing the POP3 protocol in Go, you can build applications that interact with email servers, retrieve emails, and automate various email-related tasks.

3.4 Implementing Custom Protocols

While Go's standard library provides robust support for many common network protocols, you might encounter situations where you need to create your own custom protocols.

This could be for a variety of reasons, such as

- Proprietary Applications: You might be developing a proprietary application that requires a specialized communication protocol not covered by standard protocols.

- Specialized Needs: You might have specific performance or security requirements that necessitate a custom-tailored protocol.
- Legacy Systems: You might need to interact with legacy systems that use non-standard or outdated protocols.
- IoT Devices: Communication with Internet of Things (IoT) devices often involves custom protocols designed for specific hardware or functionalities.

Implementing a custom protocol involves defining the rules, format, and semantics of the messages exchanged between applications. It's like creating your own language for your applications to communicate with each other.

Key Considerations for Custom Protocols

When designing and implementing a custom protocol, there are several key considerations

- Efficiency: Choose a data format that is efficient to encode and decode. This is particularly important for applications that require high throughput or low latency. Consider using binary formats or compressed formats to minimize the size of the messages.
- Extensibility: Design the protocol to be extensible, allowing for future additions or modifications without breaking backward compatibility. This can be achieved by using versioning or optional fields in the message format.
- Error Handling: Implement robust error handling to gracefully handle unexpected situations, such as network errors, invalid data, or protocol violations. This might involve using checksums, error codes, or retry mechanisms.
- Security: If security is a concern, consider incorporating encryption or authentication mechanisms into your

protocol. This could involve using TLS/SSL, digital signatures, or other security measures.

Steps to Implement a Custom Protocol

1. Define the Message Format: Determine the structure of the messages that will be exchanged between applications. This might involve using a text-based format like JSON or XML, or a binary format for more compact representation. Define the fields, data types, and any headers or control information that will be included in the messages.
2. Implement Encoding and Decoding: Write functions to encode and decode messages in your chosen format. Go provides various encoding and decoding packages, such as encoding/json, encoding/xml, and encoding/binary, to help you with this task.
3. Handle Connections: Use Go's net package to create sockets and handle connections. Depending on your needs, you might use TCP or UDP sockets.
4. Implement the Protocol Logic: Write the code to handle the exchange of messages according to your protocol rules. This might involve sending requests, receiving responses, and processing data according to the defined message format.
5. Error Handling and Logging: Implement robust error handling to catch and handle any errors that might occur during communication. Use logging to record important events and facilitate debugging.

Example

Let's say you're building a simple chat application where clients send messages to a server, and the server broadcasts the messages to all connected clients.

You could define a custom protocol with the following message format

```
MessageType: byte (0 for text message, 1 for join
notification, 2 for leave notification)

MessageLength: uint32 (length of the message
payload)

MessagePayload:byte (the actual message content)
```

You would then implement encoding and decoding functions to convert messages to and from this format. The server would listen for connections from clients, and each client would send messages in this format to the server. The server would then broadcast the messages to all other connected clients.

Real-World Examples

Custom protocols are used in various real-world applications, such as

- Financial Trading Systems: High-frequency trading systems often use custom protocols optimized for speed and efficiency.
- Game Servers: Online games often use custom protocols to handle real-time communication between players and the game server.
- Industrial Automation: Industrial automation systems often use custom protocols for communication between sensors, actuators, and controllers.

By understanding how to implement custom protocols in Go, you gain the flexibility to design and build network applications that meet your specific needs, whether it's for proprietary systems, specialized applications, or communication with unique devices.

Chapter 4: Working with Network Data Formats

We've explored the world of sockets, connections, and protocols, the essential building blocks of network communication. But what about the actual data that flows through these channels? How do we structure and interpret the information that travels across networks? This is where network data formats come into play.

Think of data formats as the containers we use to package information for transport. Just as you wouldn't ship fragile items without proper packaging, we need to format data appropriately before sending it over a network. This ensures that the data remains intact during transmission and that the receiving application can understand and interpret it correctly.

In this chapter, we'll explore some of the most common data formats used in network programming, including JSON, XML, and Protocol Buffers. We'll also touch upon other serialization formats that you might encounter in your network adventures.

4.1 JSON Encoding and Decoding

Let's talk about JSON, the superstar of data formats in the world of web development and beyond. JSON, or JavaScript Object Notation, has become incredibly popular for exchanging data between applications, especially in web APIs and microservices. It's a lightweight, text-based format that's both human-readable and machine-friendly.

Think of JSON as a simple and elegant way to represent data in a structured format. It's like a universal language that different applications can understand, regardless of the programming language they are written in. Whether you're sending data from a web server to a browser, or exchanging information between different microservices, JSON provides a common ground for communication.

Why JSON is So Popular

JSON's popularity stems from a few key factors

- Simplicity: JSON's syntax is straightforward and easy to learn. It uses a key-value structure, similar to dictionaries in Python or maps in Go, making it intuitive to represent data.
- Readability: JSON is human-readable, meaning you can easily understand the structure and content of the data just by looking at it. This makes it great for debugging and troubleshooting.
- Ubiquity: JSON is supported by almost every programming language and platform, making it a truly universal data format.
- Lightweight: JSON is a text-based format, so it's generally smaller in size compared to binary formats, making it efficient for network transmission.

JSON in Go

Go provides excellent support for working with JSON through its encoding/json package. This package offers a set of powerful functions for encoding Go data structures into JSON format and decoding JSON data back into Go data structures. It's your one-stop shop for all things JSON in Go.

Encoding Go Data into JSON

To transform your Go data into JSON, you use the json.Marshal() function. This function takes any Go data structure – be it a struct, a map, or even a primitive type – and converts it into a JSON-formatted byte slice. It's like taking a neatly organized box of items and creating a descriptive inventory list in JSON format.

Here's an example

Code snippet

```go
package main

import (

 "encoding/json"

 "fmt"

)


type Product struct {

 Name   string  `json:"name"`

 Price float64 `json:"price"`

}


func main() {

 p:= Product{Name: "Laptop", Price: 1299.99}

 jsonBytes, err:= json.Marshal(p)

 if err!= nil {

  fmt.Println("Error encoding JSON:",
err.Error())

  return
```

```
    }


    fmt.Println(string(jsonBytes)) // Output:
    {"name":"Laptop","price":1299.99}


}
```

In this example, we define a Product struct and create an instance of it. We then use json.Marshal() to convert this struct into a JSON-formatted byte slice. The output is a JSON string representing the product data.

Decoding JSON Data into Go

Now, let's say you receive some JSON data over a network connection, and you want to convert it into a Go data structure to work with it in your program. This is where json.Unmarshal() comes in. This function takes a byte slice containing JSON data and a pointer to a Go data structure. It then parses the JSON data and populates the fields of your Go data structure accordingly. It's like taking that inventory list and using it to unpack and organize the items back into the box.

Here's an example

```
Code snippet

package main


import (

  "encoding/json"

  "fmt"
```

```go
)


type User struct {

 Username string `json:"username"`

 Email    string `json:"email"`

}


func main() {

 jsonStr:=
`{"username":"john_doe","email":"john.doe@example
.com"}`

 var u User

 err:= json.Unmarshal(byte(jsonStr), &u)

 if err!= nil {

  fmt.Println("Error decoding JSON:",
err.Error())

  return

 }


 fmt.Println(u) // Output: {john_doe
john.doe@example.com}

}
```

In this example, we have a JSON string representing a user. We use json.Unmarshal() to decode this JSON data into a User struct.

JSON in Network Applications

JSON is widely used in network applications for various purposes, including

- Web APIs: When you interact with a web API, the data you send and receive is often in JSON format. For example, when you fetch data from a social media API, the response will likely be a JSON object containing information about users, posts, or other entities.
- Microservices Communication: In microservices architectures, where applications are broken down into smaller, independent services, JSON is often used for communication between these services.
- Configuration Files: Many applications use JSON files for configuration settings. This makes it easy to modify the application's behavior without recompiling the code.
- Data Serialization: JSON can be used to serialize data for storage or transmission. For example, you could store user data in a database in JSON format.

Advanced JSON Techniques

The encoding/json package offers more advanced features for working with JSON, including

- Customizing JSON Encoding: You can use struct tags to control how your Go data is encoded into JSON. For example, you can specify different field names, omit empty fields, or control the formatting of the output.
- Streaming JSON Data: You can stream JSON data, which is useful for handling large datasets or real-time data streams.

This allows you to process JSON data incrementally without loading the entire dataset into memory.

- Working with JSON Arrays and Objects: You can work with JSON arrays and nested objects, allowing you to represent more complex data structures.

JSON is a powerful and versatile data format that has become a cornerstone of modern web development and network programming. Go's encoding/json package provides a comprehensive set of tools for working with JSON effectively, enabling you to build robust and scalable network applications that communicate seamlessly using this popular data format.

4.2 XML Processing

While JSON has taken the web by storm with its simplicity and ease of use, XML (Extensible Markup Language) still holds a prominent position in the world of data exchange, particularly in enterprise environments and for more complex data structures. Think of XML as a more verbose, but highly structured, way to represent data. It's like a detailed blueprint with labels and annotations, providing a comprehensive and unambiguous representation of information.

XML's roots go way back, and it was designed with a focus on flexibility and extensibility. It allows you to define your own tags and structure your data in a way that makes sense for your specific needs. This makes it well-suited for representing complex data hierarchies and relationships, which is why it's often found in industries with strict data standards, like healthcare or finance.

Why XML Still Matters

Even with the rise of JSON, XML remains relevant for several reasons

- Extensibility: XML allows you to define your own tags, making it highly adaptable to various data structures and domains. This is crucial in situations where you need to represent complex data that doesn't fit neatly into predefined structures.
- Namespaces: XML supports namespaces, which allow you to avoid naming collisions when combining data from different sources. This is essential when integrating data from various systems or organizations.
- Schemas and Validation: XML has strong support for schemas, which define the rules and constraints for valid XML documents. This allows you to validate your data against a schema to ensure its integrity and conformance to specific standards.
- Legacy Systems: Many legacy systems and applications still rely on XML for data exchange. If you need to interact with these systems, understanding XML is essential.

XML in Go

Go provides excellent support for working with XML through its encoding/xml package. This package offers a set of functions for encoding Go data structures into XML format and decoding XML data back into Go data structures. It's your toolkit for navigating the world of XML in Go.

Encoding Go Data into XML

To convert your Go data structures into XML, you use the xml.Marshal() function. This function takes a Go value, typically a struct, and converts it into an XML-formatted byte slice. It's like taking a well-organized file cabinet and creating a detailed catalog of its contents in XML format.

Here's an example

```
Code snippet

package main


import (

 "encoding/xml"

 "fmt"

)


type Customer struct {

 XMLName xml.Name `xml:"customer"`

 ID       int      `xml:"id"`

 Name     string   `xml:"name"`

 Email    string   `xml:"email"`

}


func main() {

 c:= Customer{ID: 123, Name: "Jane Doe", Email:
"jane.doe@example.com"}
```

```go
xmlBytes, err := xml.Marshal(c)

if err != nil {

  fmt.Println("Error encoding XML:", err.Error())

  return

}



  fmt.Println(string(xmlBytes))

  // Output: <customer><id>123</id><name>Jane
Doe</name><email>jane.doe@example.com</email></cu
stomer>

}
```

In this example, we define a Customer struct and use xml.Marshal() to convert it into an XML-formatted byte slice. The output is an XML string representing the customer data.

Decoding XML Data into Go

When you receive XML data over a network connection, you can use xml.Unmarshal() to convert it back into a Go data structure. This function takes a byte slice containing XML data and a pointer to a Go value, typically a struct. It then parses the XML data and populates the fields of your Go value accordingly. It's like taking that XML catalog and using it to reconstruct the contents of the file cabinet.

Here's an example

```go
Code snippet

package main
```

```go
import (

  "encoding/xml"

  "fmt"

)


type Order struct {

  XMLName xml.Name `xml:"order"`

  ID       int        `xml:"id"`

  Items  Item     `xml:"items>item"`

}


type Item struct {

  XMLName xml.Name `xml:"item"`

  Name     string   `xml:"name"`

  Price    float64  `xml:"price"`

}


func main() {

  xmlStr:=  `
```

```
<order>

  <id>456</id>

  <items>

<item><name>Keyboard</name><price>79.99</price></
item>

<item><name>Mouse</name><price>29.99</price></ite
m>

  </items>

</order>
  `

var o Order

err:= xml.Unmarshal(byte(xmlStr), &o)

if err!= nil {

  fmt.Println("Error decoding XML:", err.Error())

  return

}


fmt.Println(o)

// Output: {{order} 456 [{Keyboard 79.99} {Mouse
29.99}]}

}
```

In this example, we decode an XML string representing an order into an Order struct.

XML in Network Applications

XML is commonly used in network applications for various purposes, including

- Web Services: Many web services, especially those built with SOAP (Simple Object Access Protocol), use XML for exchanging messages.
- Data Feeds: XML is often used for syndicating data feeds, such as news feeds or product catalogs.
- Configuration Files: Some applications use XML files for configuration settings, although JSON is becoming more common for this purpose.
- Data Interchange: XML is used for exchanging data between different systems or organizations, especially in industries with standardized data formats.

Advanced XML Techniques

The encoding/xml package provides more advanced features for working with XML, such as

- Namespaces and Schemas: You can work with XML namespaces to avoid naming collisions and use schemas to validate XML documents against predefined rules.
- Customizing XML Encoding: You can use struct tags to control how your Go data is encoded into XML, similar to how you customize JSON encoding. This allows you to specify XML element names, attributes, and other formatting options.
- Streaming XML Data: You can stream XML data, which is useful for handling large XML documents or real-time XML

streams. This allows you to process XML data incrementally without loading the entire document into memory.

XML, while perhaps not as trendy as JSON, remains a powerful and versatile data format for representing and exchanging complex data. Go's encoding/xml package provides a comprehensive set of tools for working with XML effectively, enabling you to build robust and interoperable network applications that can communicate with a wide range of systems and services.

4.3 Protocol Buffers

Let's explore Protocol Buffers, often affectionately called Protobuf. This is a powerful mechanism for serializing structured data, meaning it allows you to take your data structures and convert them into a format that can be easily stored or transmitted. What sets Protobuf apart is its efficiency and focus on structure. It's like having a specialized container for your data that's both compact and well-organized.

Protobuf was developed by Google and is used extensively in their internal systems and APIs. It's designed to be language-agnostic, meaning you can use it with various programming languages, making it perfect for situations where different systems need to communicate.

Why Protobuf?

Protobuf offers several advantages over other data formats like JSON or XML

- Efficiency: Protobuf uses a binary format, which is much more compact than text-based formats like JSON or XML. This means smaller message sizes, faster transmission, and reduced storage requirements. It's like sending a package via express delivery instead of regular mail.

- Structure: Protobuf enforces a structured format for your data. You define the structure of your data using a special language called Protocol Buffer Language (proto language), and this structure is then used to generate code in various programming languages. This ensures that your data is always well-defined and consistent.
- Speed: Protobuf is generally faster to encode and decode than JSON or XML. This is because the binary format is simpler to parse and process.
- Backward Compatibility: Protobuf is designed with backward compatibility in mind. You can add new fields to your data structures without breaking existing applications that use older versions of the structure. This makes it easier to evolve your data formats over time.

Defining Protobuf Messages

To work with Protobuf, you first need to define the structure of your data using the proto language. This is done in a file with a .proto extension. In this file, you define *messages*, which are like blueprints for your data structures. Each message contains fields with specific data types.

Here's an example of a .proto file defining a simple User message

```
Protocol Buffers

syntax = "proto3";



message User {
```

```
string name = 1;

int32 id = 2;

string email = 3;
```

}

This defines a message called User with three fields: name (string), id (integer), and email (string). Each field is assigned a unique number (1, 2, 3), which is used for efficient encoding.

Generating Go Code

Once you have defined your Protobuf messages in a .proto file, you need to generate Go code from it. This is done using the protoc compiler, which is the Protobuf compiler. You'll also need the Go Protobuf plugin to generate Go-specific code.

The generated Go code will contain data structures that correspond to your Protobuf messages, as well as functions for encoding and decoding these messages.

Encoding and Decoding Protobuf Messages

The generated Go code provides Marshal() and Unmarshal() functions, similar to what we saw with JSON and XML.

- proto.Marshal(): This function takes a Protobuf message object and converts it into a binary-encoded byte slice, ready to be sent over the network or stored.
- proto.Unmarshal(): This function takes a binary-encoded byte slice and a pointer to a Protobuf message object. It decodes the binary data and populates the fields of the message object.

Example

Code snippet

```go
// Assuming you have the Go code generated from
the User.proto file


package main


import (

  "fmt"

  "github.com/golang/protobuf/proto" // Import the
Go Protobuf package

)


func main() {

  // Create a User message

  user:= &User{

   Name:   "Bob",

   Id:     42,

   Email: "bob@example.com",

  }
```

```go
// Encode the message into a byte slice

data, err := proto.Marshal(user)

if err != nil {

  fmt.Println("Error encoding Protobuf:",
err.Error())

    return

}


//... send the 'data' byte slice over the
network...


// On the receiving end, decode the message

newUser := &User{}

err = proto.Unmarshal(data, newUser)

if err != nil {

  fmt.Println("Error decoding Protobuf:",
err.Error())

    return

}


fmt.Println(newUser) // Output: name:"Bob" id:42
email:"bob@example.com"
```

}

Real-World Examples

Protobuf is used in a wide variety of applications where efficiency and structure are paramount

- Microservices Communication: Many microservices-based systems use Protobuf for communication between services due to its performance and cross-language support.
- gRPC: gRPC, a high-performance RPC framework, uses Protobuf as its default message format.
- Data Storage: Protobuf can be used to efficiently store structured data in files or databases.
- Networked Applications: Applications that require low latency and high throughput, such as online games or real-time streaming applications, often benefit from Protobuf's efficiency.

By understanding and utilizing Protobuf, you can significantly enhance the performance and efficiency of your network applications, especially those that involve frequent data exchange or require interoperability between different systems.

4.4 Other Data Serialization Formats

While JSON, XML, and Protobuf are some of the most popular data serialization formats used in network programming, they are by no means the only options. Depending on the specific needs of your application, you might encounter or choose to use other formats that offer different trade-offs in terms of performance, readability, compactness, or features.

Let's explore a few of these alternative formats

MessagePack

MessagePack is a binary serialization format that aims to be more compact and efficient than JSON. It's like a super-efficient packing algorithm that can squeeze your data into a smaller space, making it ideal for situations where bandwidth or storage is limited. MessagePack supports a wide range of data types, including primitive types, arrays, maps, and even custom data structures.

One of the key advantages of MessagePack is its performance. It's generally faster to encode and decode than JSON, thanks to its binary format, which is simpler and quicker to parse. This makes it a good choice for applications that require high throughput or low latency.

Another advantage of MessagePack is its cross-platform compatibility. It's supported by a wide range of programming languages, making it suitable for exchanging data between different systems.

YAML

YAML (YAML Ain't Markup Language) is a human-readable data serialization format that is often used for configuration files.[1] It's designed to be easy for humans to read and write, with a minimal amount of syntax. YAML is often preferred over JSON or XML for configuration files because it's less verbose and more concise.

YAML supports a variety of data structures, including lists, maps, and scalar values. It also allows you to add comments to your data, which can be helpful for documentation purposes.

CSV

CSV (Comma-Separated Values) is a simple, text-based format for representing tabular data. It's essentially a table of values where each row is represented by a line of text, and the values in each row are separated by commas. CSV is widely used for exchanging data between spreadsheets and databases.

While CSV is simple and easy to understand, it has some limitations. It doesn't support complex data structures, and it can be ambiguous if the data contains commas or other special characters.

Apache Avro

Apache Avro is a binary serialization format that is often used in big data applications. It's schema-based, meaning that the schema of the data is included with the data itself. This allows Avro to be self-describing and enables efficient data processing.

Avro supports a wide range of data types and offers features like schema evolution, which allows you to modify the schema without breaking compatibility with existing data.

Apache Thrift

Apache Thrift is a cross-language serialization framework developed by Facebook. It allows you to define data structures and services in a language-agnostic way and then generate code for various programming languages. Thrift supports various transport protocols and serialization formats, making it a versatile choice for building distributed systems.

Choosing the Right Format

The choice of which data serialization format to use depends on the specific needs of your application.

Here are some factors to consider

- Performance: If performance is critical, consider using a binary format like MessagePack or Protobuf.

- Readability: If humans need to read and understand the data, consider using a human-readable format like JSON or YAML.
- Compactness: If minimizing the size of the data is important, consider using a compact format like MessagePack or Protobuf.
- Interoperability: If you need to exchange data with systems written in other programming languages, consider using a language-agnostic format like JSON, Protobuf, or Apache Thrift.
- Features: Consider the specific features offered by each format, such as schema support, extensibility, or backward compatibility.

By carefully considering these factors, you can choose the data serialization format that best suits your application's requirements and ensures efficient and reliable data exchange.

Chapter 5: Building Client-Server Applications

These are the workhorses of the networked world, powering everything from web browsing and email to online games and financial trading systems.

Think of client-server applications as a conversation between two parties. The client initiates the conversation, makes requests, and receives responses. The server, on the other hand, listens for requests, processes them, and sends back the appropriate responses. It's a classic dynamic that forms the backbone of countless applications we use every day.

In this chapter, we'll explore the core concepts of client-server architectures, delve into connection management techniques, and emphasize the importance of robust error handling. And to top it off, we'll build a simple chat application to demonstrate these concepts in action.

5.1 Client-Server Architectures

Let's explore the world of client-server architectures, a fundamental concept in network programming and the backbone of countless applications we use every day. Think of it as a partnership, a collaboration between two distinct entities with different roles and responsibilities.

In this partnership, the client is typically the application that the user interacts with directly. It could be a web browser, a mobile app, a desktop application, or even a smart device. The client's primary job is to provide a user-friendly interface, gather input from the user, and present the results of requests made to the server.

The server, on the other hand, is the behind-the-scenes workhorse. It's often a powerful machine or a cluster of machines running in a data center. The server's role is to listen for requests from clients, process those requests, perform any necessary computations or data retrieval, and send back the appropriate responses.

This division of labor, this clear separation of concerns, is what makes client-server architectures so powerful and versatile. It allows us to build complex applications by breaking them down into smaller, more manageable components.

Benefits of Client-Server Architectures

There are several key benefits to using a client-server approach

- Centralized Logic and Data: The server acts as a central point of control, managing data and resources efficiently. This ensures data consistency and integrity, as all clients access the same data source. It also simplifies maintenance and updates, as changes can be made on the server without affecting the clients.
- Scalability: Client-server architectures are inherently scalable. As the number of clients increases, you can scale up the server by adding more processing power, memory, or storage. You can even distribute the load across multiple servers to handle a massive number of clients.
- Flexibility and Reusability: The server can provide a common set of services and resources to a variety of clients, regardless of their platform or operating system. This promotes code reusability and simplifies development.
- Security: By centralizing data and logic on the server, you can implement robust security measures to protect sensitive information. This includes access control, authentication, and encryption.

Types of Client-Server Architectures

Client-server architectures come in various flavors, each tailored to specific needs and complexities

- Two-Tier Architecture: This is the most basic form, consisting of just two layers: the client and the server. The client handles the user interface and application logic, while the server manages the data storage and retrieval. This architecture is suitable for simple applications with limited scalability requirements.
- Three-Tier Architecture: This architecture introduces an intermediate layer between the client and the server, often called the application server. This middle layer handles business logic and data processing, offloading some of the work from the server and improving performance. This architecture is common in web applications, where the application server handles tasks like user authentication, session management, and data validation.
- N-Tier Architecture: This is an extension of the three-tier architecture, where additional layers are added to further distribute tasks and improve scalability. These layers might include web servers, caching servers, load balancers, or security layers. N-tier architectures are used for complex, high-performance applications that require a high degree of flexibility and scalability.

Choosing the Right Architecture

The choice of which client-server architecture to use depends on several factors

- Complexity of the Application: Simple applications with limited functionality might be well-served by a two-tier architecture. More complex applications with multiple layers of logic and data processing might require a three-tier or N-tier architecture.

- Scalability Requirements: If you anticipate a large number of clients or a high volume of data, you'll need an architecture that can scale effectively. Three-tier and N-tier architectures are generally more scalable than two-tier architectures.
- Performance Goals: The architecture can significantly impact the performance of your application. Multi-tier architectures can improve performance by distributing the load and utilizing caching mechanisms.
- Security Needs: If your application handles sensitive data, you'll need an architecture that provides robust security features. Centralizing data and logic on the server allows you to implement strong security measures.

Real-World Examples

Client-server architectures are ubiquitous in the modern world.

Here are a few examples

- Web Browsing: When you access a website, your web browser (the client) sends requests to the web server, which processes the requests and sends back the HTML, CSS, and JavaScript that make up the web page.
- Email: When you send an email, your email client connects to an SMTP server (the server) to send the email, and the recipient's email client connects to a POP3 or IMAP server to retrieve the email.
- Online Games: Online games typically use a client-server architecture, where the game client runs on the player's machine and communicates with a game server that

manages the game state and coordinates interactions between players.

- Financial Trading Systems: Financial trading systems rely on client-server architectures to provide real-time access to market data and execute trades.

By understanding the principles of client-server architectures and the various types of architectures available, you can make informed decisions about how to design and build your network applications to meet your specific needs and goals.

5.2 Connection Management

In the world of client-server applications, connections are the lifeblood of communication. They are the channels through which clients and servers exchange data, requests, and responses. Think of them as the telephone lines that keep the conversation going. Efficient connection management is crucial for ensuring the smooth and reliable operation of these applications.

Just like a good conversation requires clear communication and attentive listening, effective connection management involves several key aspects:

Connection Establishment

Before any data can be exchanged, a connection needs to be established between the client and the server. This process is like the initial handshake that starts a conversation. For TCP connections, this involves a three-way handshake, where the client and server exchange synchronization and acknowledgment messages to ensure they are both ready to communicate.

In Go, the net.Dial() function on the client-side initiates this handshake, reaching out to the server's listening socket. On the server-side, the Accept() method on the listener object accepts the connection request, establishing a dedicated communication channel between the client and the server.

Connection Persistence

Once a connection is established, it can be kept open for multiple requests and responses. This is known as connection persistence, and it can significantly improve performance by avoiding the overhead of establishing a new connection for each request. Imagine having to redial a phone number every time you wanted to say something in a conversation - it would be quite inefficient!

HTTP/1.1, the protocol that powers most web traffic, supports persistent connections by default. This means that a web browser can send multiple requests to a web server over the same connection, reducing latency and improving responsiveness.

Connection Pooling

In situations where many clients need to connect to the same server, creating a new connection for each client can be resource-intensive. This is where connection pooling comes in. A connection pool is like a shared pool of resources, where clients can borrow and return connections as needed.

Think of it like a car rental service. Instead of each client buying their own car, they can rent one from the pool when they need it and return it when they're done. This reduces the overall cost and ensures that resources are used efficiently.

In Go, you can implement connection pooling using various techniques, such as channels or third-party libraries. The key idea is to maintain a set of open connections to the server and allow clients to reuse these connections, avoiding the overhead of establishing new connections for each request.

Connection Termination

Just as a conversation ends with a polite farewell, a network connection needs to be terminated properly when it's no longer needed. This involves closing the connection from both the client and the server-side, ensuring that any pending data is transmitted and that both parties are aware that the conversation is over.

In Go, the Close() method on the net.Conn object is used to close a connection. It's important to handle disconnections gracefully, especially in cases of unexpected network errors or application crashes, to prevent data loss or corruption.

Go's Concurrency Features: Handling Multiple Conversations

Go's built-in concurrency features, such as goroutines and channels, make it particularly well-suited for managing connections in client-server applications. Goroutines allow you to handle each client connection in its own lightweight thread, preventing one slow or blocked connection from affecting others. Channels provide a safe and efficient way for goroutines to communicate and synchronize their actions.

Real-World Examples

Connection management plays a critical role in many real-world applications

- Web Servers: Web servers handle a large number of concurrent connections from users browsing the web. Efficient connection management is crucial for ensuring that the server can handle the load and provide a responsive experience to users.
- Database Servers: Database servers manage connections from multiple applications accessing the database.

Connection pooling is often used to improve performance and reduce the overhead of establishing new connections.

- Messaging Applications: Messaging applications like WhatsApp or Telegram need to manage persistent connections to their servers to deliver messages in real-time.
- Online Games: Online games require low-latency connections to provide a smooth and responsive gaming experience. Connection management techniques are used to minimize lag and ensure that players can interact with the game world seamlessly.

By mastering the art of connection management in Go, you can build high-performance, reliable, and scalable client-server applications that can handle the demands of the modern networked world.

5.3 Error Handling

In the world of network programming, things don't always go as planned. Network connections can be flaky, servers can become overloaded, and data can get lost or corrupted in transit. That's why robust error handling is absolutely crucial for building reliable and resilient client-server applications. Think of it as your application's safety net, ensuring that it can gracefully handle unexpected situations and recover from errors without crashing or disrupting the user experience.

Types of Network Errors

Network errors can manifest in various ways, but they can be broadly classified into a few common categories

Connection Errors

These errors occur when establishing or terminating a connection.

Examples include

- Connection Refused: The server might be down, unreachable, or not listening on the specified port.
- Connection Timeout: The connection attempt might take too long to complete, indicating a network issue or an unresponsive server.
- Connection Reset: The connection might be abruptly closed by the server or due to a network problem.

Data Errors

These errors occur during the transmission of data.

Examples include

- Data Corruption: The data might be altered or corrupted during transmission due to network noise or other factors.
- Incomplete Data: The application might receive only a partial chunk of data, leading to inconsistencies or unexpected behavior.
- Invalid Data Format: The received data might not conform to the expected format, such as invalid JSON or XML, causing parsing errors.

Server Errors

These errors originate from the server-side of the application.

Examples include

- Server Overload: The server might be overwhelmed with requests, leading to slow response times or errors.
- Database Errors: Problems with the database, such as connection failures or query errors, can cause server-side errors.
- Application Crashes: Bugs or unexpected conditions in the server application can lead to crashes, disrupting service to clients.

Effective Error Handling Strategies

Handling errors effectively involves a combination of proactive and reactive measures

- Detecting Errors: The first step is to be vigilant in detecting errors. Most network operations in Go return an error value. Always check this value after every network call. Don't assume that everything will always work perfectly!
- Handling Errors Gracefully: Once an error is detected, handle it gracefully. This might involve:
    - Retrying the Operation: For transient errors, such as temporary network issues, retrying the operation might be successful.
    - Logging the Error: Record the error details for debugging and analysis. This can help you identify patterns and improve your application's resilience.
    - Providing User Feedback: If the error affects the user experience, display an informative message to the user, explaining the situation and suggesting possible actions.
    - Failing Fast: For critical errors that cannot be recovered from, it's sometimes better to fail fast and terminate the application or connection to prevent further damage or inconsistencies.
- Preventing Cascading Failures: When handling errors, it's important to prevent them from cascading through your application and causing widespread disruption. Isolate errors and handle them locally to minimize their impact.

Go's Error Handling Mechanisms

Go provides several mechanisms for handling errors effectively

- Error Values: As mentioned earlier, most network functions in Go return an error value. You can check this value using an if statement and take appropriate action based on the error type.
- Custom Error Types: You can define your own error types to provide more context and information about specific errors. This can help you differentiate between different types of errors and handle them more effectively.
- Panic and Recover: For unrecoverable errors, you can use the panic() function to terminate the program abruptly. This is useful for situations where continuing execution would lead to unpredictable or undesirable behavior. The recover() function can be used to regain control after a panic and perform cleanup operations before the program terminates.

Real-World Examples

Error handling is critical in various real-world network applications

- Web Servers: Web servers need to handle errors gracefully to avoid crashing or disrupting service to users. They might display error pages, retry failed requests, or log errors for later analysis.
- Online Games: Online games need to handle network errors to prevent players from being disconnected or losing progress. They might implement reconnection mechanisms or provide fallback options in case of network issues.

- Financial Trading Systems: In financial trading systems, even small errors can have significant consequences. Robust error handling is essential to prevent financial losses and ensure the integrity of the system.

By incorporating thorough error handling into your Go network applications, you can create robust and reliable systems that can withstand the challenges of the networked world and provide a smooth and dependable experience for your users. Remember, error handling is not just about preventing crashes; it's about building resilience and ensuring that your applications can gracefully handle the unexpected.

5.4 Example

Let's put our knowledge of client-server architectures, connection management, and error handling into practice by building a simple chat application. This application will allow multiple clients to connect to a server and exchange messages in real-time. It's a classic example that demonstrates the core principles of client-server communication and provides a foundation for building more complex network applications.

Server Code

Code snippet

```
package main


import (

  "fmt"

  "net"
```

```go
)


// This function handles a single client
connection

func handleClient(conn net.Conn, clients
map[net.Conn]bool) {

  defer conn.Close() // Ensure the connection is
closed when the function exits

  clients[conn] = true // Add the client to the
list of connected clients


  // Read messages from the client and broadcast
them to other clients
  buffer:= make(byte, 1024)

  for {

    n, err:= conn.Read(buffer)

    if err!= nil {

      fmt.Println("Error reading:", err.Error())

      delete(clients, conn) // Remove the client
from the list

      return

    }
```

```go
  // Broadcast the message to all connected
clients

  for client:= range clients {

    if client!= conn { // Don't send the message
back to the sender

      _, err:= client.Write(buffer[:n])

      if err!= nil {

        fmt.Println("Error writing:", err.Error())

      }

    }

  }

}


func main() {

 // Listen on TCP port 8080

 listener, err:= net.Listen("tcp", ":8080")

 if err!= nil {

  fmt.Println("Error listening:", err.Error())

  return

 }
```

```go
defer listener.Close()

fmt.Println("Chat server started on:8080")

// Keep track of connected clients
clients := make(map[net.Conn]bool)

// Accept and handle client connections
for {
    conn, err := listener.Accept()
    if err != nil {
        fmt.Println("Error accepting connection:",
err.Error())
        continue
    }

    // Handle the client in a new goroutine
    go handleClient(conn, clients)
}
}
```

In this server code

- We create a TCP listener on port 8080.
- We use a map to keep track of connected clients.
- The handleClient function handles each client connection in a separate goroutine.
- It reads messages from the client and broadcasts them to all other connected clients.

Client Code

Code snippet

```
package main


import (

  "bufio"

  "fmt"

  "net"

  "os"

)


func main() {

 // Connect to the server

 conn, err:= net.Dial("tcp", "localhost:8080")

 if err!= nil {
```

```go
        fmt.Println("Error connecting:", err.Error())

        return

    }

    defer conn.Close()


    fmt.Println("Connected to chat server")


    // Handle user input and sending messages

    go func() {

        reader:= bufio.NewReader(os.Stdin)

        for {

            message, _:= reader.ReadString('\n')

            conn.Write(byte(message))

        }

    }()


    // Receive and print messages from the server

    buffer:= make(byte, 1024)

    for {

        n, err:= conn.Read(buffer)
```

```
if err!= nil {

  fmt.Println("Error reading:", err.Error())

  return

}



  fmt.Print(string(buffer[:n]))

 }

}
```

In this client code

- We connect to the server on localhost:8080.
- We use a goroutine to continuously read user input and send it to the server.
- We also continuously read messages from the server and print them to the console.

Running the Chat Application

1. Save the server code as server.go and the client code as client.go.
2. Run the server: go run server.go
3. Open multiple terminals and run the client in each: go run client.go
4. Now you can type messages in each client terminal, and they will be broadcast to all other connected clients.

This simple chat application demonstrates the core concepts of client-server communication, including

- Connection Establishment and Management: The client connects to the server, and the server manages multiple client connections concurrently.
- Data Exchange: Clients send messages to the server, and the server broadcasts them to other clients.
- Concurrency: The server handles multiple clients concurrently using goroutines.

This example provides a solid foundation for building more complex and feature-rich chat applications or other types of client-server applications. You can extend this example by adding features like user authentication, private messaging, or file sharing.

Chapter 6: Concurrent Network Programming

Concurrency is like having multiple workers in a factory, each performing a task independently, allowing you to achieve more in less time.

In this chapter, we'll explore Go's concurrency primitives: goroutines and channels. We'll see how they can be used to build highly efficient and scalable network applications that can handle thousands of concurrent connections with ease. We'll also discuss the challenges of concurrency, such as race conditions, and how to avoid them. And to bring it all together, we'll build a concurrent web server that can handle multiple requests simultaneously.

6.1 Goroutines and Concurrency

Let's explore one of the most powerful features of Go: goroutines. These are the secret sauce that makes Go so well-suited for concurrent programming, especially in the realm of network applications. Think of goroutines as lightweight threads, like tiny, independent workers within your program, each capable of executing tasks concurrently without stepping on each other's toes.

What makes goroutines so special is their efficiency. Unlike traditional operating system threads, which can be quite resource-intensive, goroutines are incredibly lightweight. They have a very small memory footprint and can be created and destroyed with minimal overhead. This allows you to create thousands, even millions, of goroutines without bogging down your system. It's like having an army of ants, each carrying a small load, working together to accomplish a larger task.

Creating Goroutines

Creating a goroutine is remarkably simple. You just add the go keyword before a function call, and voilà! You've launched a new, independent worker. It's like saying, "Hey, you go take care of this while I continue with my work."

Here's an example

Code snippet

```
package main

import (

    "fmt"

    "time"

)

func printNumbers() {

    for i:= 1; i <= 5; i++ {

        fmt.Println(i)

        time.Sleep(time.Millisecond
* 500)
```

```go
        }

    }

    func main() {

            go printNumbers() // Launch a new
    goroutine to print numbers

            fmt.Println("Hello from main
    goroutine!")

            time.Sleep(time.Second * 3)

    }
```

In this example, the printNumbers function is executed in a separate goroutine. The main function continues to execute concurrently, printing "Hello from main goroutine!" and then waiting for 3 seconds. Meanwhile, the printNumbers goroutine happily prints numbers from 1 to 5 with a delay of 500 milliseconds between each number.

Benefits of Goroutines

Goroutines bring several benefits to the table

- Efficiency: Their lightweight nature allows you to create a massive number of them without significant performance overhead. This makes them ideal for handling concurrent tasks, such as managing multiple network connections.

- Simplicity: Creating goroutines is incredibly easy, requiring just the go keyword. This reduces the complexity of concurrent programming and makes it more accessible.
- Scalability: Goroutines enable you to build highly scalable applications that can handle a large number of concurrent operations. This is particularly important for network applications that need to serve many clients simultaneously.
- Responsiveness: By offloading tasks to goroutines, you can keep your main application responsive, even when performing time-consuming operations. This is crucial for providing a smooth user experience.

Real-World Examples

Goroutines are used extensively in real-world Go applications, particularly those that involve networking or concurrency:

- Web Servers: High-performance web servers like those used by Netflix and Dropbox utilize goroutines to handle thousands of concurrent client requests. Each request is processed in its own goroutine, ensuring that one slow request doesn't block others.
- Messaging Systems: Real-time messaging applications like Slack and Discord rely on goroutines to manage connections to multiple users and deliver messages efficiently.
- Data Pipelines: Goroutines are used in data pipelines to process data concurrently, improving throughput and reducing latency.
- Concurrent Algorithms: Many concurrent algorithms and data structures are implemented using goroutines, enabling efficient parallel processing.

By mastering goroutines, you unlock a powerful tool for building concurrent and scalable network applications in Go. They provide an elegant and efficient way to manage multiple tasks simultaneously, making your applications more responsive, robust, and capable of handling the demands of the modern networked world.

6.2 Channels and Communication

We've explored the power of goroutines, those lightweight threads that allow us to perform tasks concurrently. But concurrency without communication is like a group of musicians playing different tunes without a conductor. It can lead to chaos and disharmony. That's where channels come in.

Channels are the communication highways of Go's concurrency model. They provide a safe and efficient way for goroutines to exchange data and synchronize their actions. Think of them as pipes that connect goroutines, allowing them to send and receive values without the risk of race conditions or data corruption.

Creating Channels

Creating a channel is as simple as using the make() function with the chan keyword, followed by the type of data the channel will carry. For example, to create a channel that carries integers:

Code snippet

```
ch:= make(chan int)
```

This creates a channel named ch that can be used to send and receive integer values.

Sending and Receiving Data

To send a value on a channel, use the <- operator, with the channel on the left and the value on the right

Code snippet

```
ch <- 42 // Send the value 42 on the channel
ch
```

To receive a value from a channel, use the <- operator with the channel on the right

Code snippet

```
value:= <-ch // Receive a value from the
channel ch and store it in value
```

Buffered and Unbuffered Channels

Channels can be either buffered or unbuffered.

- Unbuffered Channels: In an unbuffered channel, the sender blocks until a receiver is ready to receive the value. It's like a direct handoff, where the sender waits until the receiver is there to take the item. This provides tight synchronization between goroutines.
- Buffered Channels: A buffered channel, on the other hand, has a capacity to hold a certain number of values. The sender can send values without blocking as long as the buffer is not full. It's like having a mailbox where the sender can drop off multiple letters without waiting for the recipient to pick them up. This allows for more asynchronous communication between goroutines.

To create a buffered channel, specify the buffer size as the second argument to the make() function

Code snippet

```
ch:= make(chan int, 10) // Create a buffered
channel with a capacity of 10 integers
```

Benefits of Channels

Channels bring several benefits to concurrent programming

- Safety: Channels provide a safe way for goroutines to communicate and share data. They ensure that only one goroutine can access the channel at a time, preventing race conditions and data corruption.
- Efficiency: Channels are optimized for performance and can handle high volumes of data exchange between goroutines.
- Synchronization: Channels can be used to synchronize the execution of goroutines. For example, a goroutine can wait to receive a value on a channel, effectively blocking until another goroutine sends a value, ensuring that certain operations happen in a specific order.

Real-World Examples

Channels are used extensively in real-world Go applications to manage concurrency and communication

- Producer-Consumer Pattern: Channels are often used to implement the producer-consumer pattern, where one or more goroutines produce data and send it on a channel, while other goroutines consume the data from the channel. This pattern is common in data processing and streaming applications.

- Worker Pools: Channels can be used to create worker pools, where a set of goroutines are waiting to receive tasks from a channel. This allows you to distribute work among multiple workers and improve efficiency.
- Event Broadcasting: Channels can be used to broadcast events to multiple goroutines. For example, a server can use a channel to notify all connected clients about a new message or event.
- Timeout and Cancellation: Channels can be used to implement timeout and cancellation mechanisms. For example, a goroutine can wait for a value on a channel with a timeout, or it can be canceled by closing the channel.

By mastering channels, you gain a powerful tool for managing concurrency and communication in your Go applications. They provide an elegant and efficient way to coordinate the actions of goroutines and ensure safe and reliable data exchange, making your applications more robust and scalable.

6.3 Handling Multiple Connections

One of the most powerful applications of Go's concurrency model in network programming is handling multiple connections simultaneously. Think of a bustling server, receiving requests from numerous clients all over the world. Without concurrency, the server would have to handle each request one by one, leading to slow response times and a poor user experience. But with Go's goroutines and channels, we can build servers that effortlessly handle a multitude of connections, ensuring responsiveness and efficiency.

The Challenge of Multiple Connections

Imagine a web server receiving requests from hundreds or even thousands of users simultaneously. Each request might involve fetching data from a database, processing information, and generating a response. If the server handles these requests sequentially, one request at a time, the users would experience significant delays, and the server could easily become overwhelmed.

This is where concurrency comes to the rescue. By utilizing goroutines, we can delegate each incoming connection to its own lightweight thread of execution. This allows the server to process multiple connections concurrently, ensuring that one slow or long-running request doesn't hold up the others. It's like having a team of dedicated waiters in a restaurant, each serving a table independently, ensuring that all customers receive prompt service.

Goroutines to the Rescue

In Go, handling multiple connections concurrently is remarkably straightforward. When the server accepts a new connection, it simply launches a new goroutine to handle that connection. This goroutine can then perform all the necessary tasks for that connection, such as reading data, processing the request, and sending a response, without blocking the main server process.

Here's a basic example of a concurrent TCP server

Code snippet

```
func handleConnection(conn net.Conn) {

    defer conn.Close()

    //... read data from the connection, process
it, and send a response...
```

```go
}


func main() {

    listener, err:= net.Listen("tcp", ":8080")

    //... handle error...

    for {

        conn, err:= listener.Accept()

        //... handle error...

        go handleConnection(conn) // Handle each
connection in a new goroutine

    }

}
```

In this example, the handleConnection function is responsible for handling a single client connection. The main function listens for incoming connections and, for each connection, launches a new goroutine to execute handleConnection. This allows the server to handle multiple connections concurrently without blocking.

Channels for Coordination

While goroutines provide the concurrency, channels can be used to coordinate and communicate between these concurrent processes. For example, you might use a channel to signal when a connection is closed or to send data between different goroutines handling different aspects of the connection.

Benefits of Concurrent Connection Handling

Handling multiple connections concurrently offers several benefits

- Improved Responsiveness: Clients experience faster response times as their requests are processed concurrently, even if other requests are still being processed.
- Increased Throughput: The server can handle a larger number of requests per unit of time, improving overall throughput and efficiency.
- Enhanced Scalability: Concurrent servers can scale more effectively to handle increasing client demand, as they can utilize multiple processor cores and distribute the workload across multiple goroutines.
- Resource Efficiency: Goroutines are lightweight, so creating a large number of them doesn't consume excessive resources.

Real-World Examples

Concurrent connection handling is essential in various real-world applications

- Web Servers: Modern web servers, like those used by Google and Amazon, handle millions of concurrent connections from users browsing the web. Concurrency is crucial for providing a responsive and scalable web experience.
- Chat Applications: Chat applications need to handle multiple connections from users sending and receiving messages in real-time. Goroutines and channels enable efficient message delivery and user interaction.

- Game Servers: Online games often involve a large number of players interacting concurrently. Game servers utilize concurrency to manage player connections, update game state, and handle game logic.
- Financial Trading Systems: Financial trading systems require low latency and high throughput to process trades quickly and efficiently. Concurrent connection handling is essential for meeting these performance demands.

By mastering the techniques of concurrent connection handling in Go, you can build high-performance, scalable, and responsive network applications that can handle the demands of the modern digital world. Goroutines and channels provide the foundation for building concurrent systems that can efficiently manage a multitude of connections and provide a seamless experience for your users.

6.4 Avoiding Race Conditions

Concurrency in Go, with its goroutines and channels, is a powerful tool for building high-performance network applications. However, it also introduces a new set of challenges, particularly the risk of race conditions. Think of a race condition like two people trying to edit the same document simultaneously. The end result can be a jumbled mess, with neither person's changes fully reflected.

In concurrent programming, a race condition occurs when two or more goroutines access and modify the same shared data concurrently, leading to unpredictable and often incorrect behavior. The outcome depends on the exact timing and order in which the goroutines execute, making these bugs notoriously difficult to track down and debug.

Understanding the Dangers of Race Conditions

Imagine a simple counter variable shared between multiple goroutines. Each goroutine might increment the counter by one.

Seems simple enough, right? But without proper synchronization, the following scenario can occur

1. Goroutine 1 reads the current value of the counter, let's say it's 10.
2. Goroutine 2 also reads the current value of the counter, which is still 10.
3. Goroutine 1 increments its local copy of the counter to 11.
4. Goroutine 2 also increments its local copy of the counter to 11.
5. Goroutine 1 writes its updated value (11) back to the shared counter.
6. Goroutine 2 also writes its updated value (11) back to the shared counter.

The end result? The counter is incremented only once, to 11, instead of twice, to 12. This might seem like a minor issue, but in complex applications, race conditions can lead to data corruption, crashes, and unpredictable behavior, making them a serious concern.

Synchronization to the Rescue

To avoid race conditions, we need to synchronize access to shared data. Synchronization ensures that only one goroutine can access and modify the shared data at a time, preventing conflicts and ensuring data consistency.

Go provides several powerful tools for synchronization

- Mutexes: A mutex (mutual exclusion) is like a lock that protects a shared resource. Only one goroutine can hold the lock at a time. Any other goroutine that tries to acquire the lock will be blocked until the lock is released. This ensures that only one goroutine can access the shared[1] data at any given time.
- Go's sync package provides the Mutex type for this purpose.

Here's a simple example

```
Code snippet



import (


  "fmt"


  "sync"


  "time"


)



type Counter struct {
```

```go
    mu      sync.Mutex

    value int

}

func (c *Counter) Increment() {

  c.mu.Lock() // Acquire the lock

  defer c.mu.Unlock() // Ensure the lock is
released

  c.value++

}

func main() {

  counter := Counter{}

  for i := 0; i < 1000; i++ {

    go counter.Increment()
```

```
    }


    time.Sleep(time.Millisecond * 100) // Wait
    for goroutines to finish


    fmt.Println(counter.value) // Should print
    1000


}
```

In this example, the Increment method uses a mutex to protect the value field from concurrent access.

- Channels: Channels, besides being excellent communication tools, can also be used for synchronization. By sending and receiving values on a channel, you can control the order in which goroutines execute and ensure that certain operations happen in a specific sequence.
- Atomic Operations: For simple operations on basic data types, like integers or booleans, you can use atomic operations provided by the sync/atomic package. These operations are performed atomically, meaning they are indivisible and cannot be interrupted by other goroutines.

Best Practices for Avoiding Race Conditions

Here are some general guidelines to help you avoid race conditions

- Minimize Shared Data: The less shared data you have, the fewer opportunities for race conditions. Try to encapsulate data within goroutines and use channels for communication instead of sharing data directly.
- Use Synchronization Primitives: Whenever you need to access shared data from multiple goroutines, use appropriate synchronization primitives like mutexes or channels to protect the data.
- Keep Critical Sections Short: The code blocks protected by synchronization primitives (critical sections) should be as short as possible to minimize contention and improve performance.
- Test Concurrently: Testing your code with multiple goroutines can help you uncover race conditions that might not be apparent during sequential execution. Go provides tools like the -race flag for the go command to help detect race conditions during testing.

Real-World Implications

Race conditions can have serious consequences in real-world applications

- Data Corruption: In applications that deal with sensitive data, like financial transactions or medical records, race conditions can lead to data corruption, causing inconsistencies and potentially significant harm.

- Application Crashes: Race conditions can cause unexpected behavior and crashes, disrupting service and leading to user frustration.
- Security Vulnerabilities: In some cases, race conditions can be exploited by attackers to gain unauthorized access to data or systems.

By understanding the dangers of race conditions and applying proper synchronization techniques, you can build concurrent Go applications that are not only efficient but also safe and reliable. Remember, concurrency is a powerful tool, but it needs to be wielded with care and attention to detail.

6.5 Example

Let's solidify our understanding of concurrency in Go by building a concurrent web server. This server will be able to handle multiple requests simultaneously, showcasing the power of goroutines and channels in a real-world scenario.

The Need for Concurrency in Web Servers

Imagine a web server receiving a surge of requests, perhaps during a flash sale or a popular product launch. If the server processes these requests one by one, users would experience frustrating delays, and the server could become overwhelmed, potentially leading to crashes or downtime.

To avoid this, we can leverage Go's concurrency model. By using goroutines, we can handle each incoming request in its own lightweight thread of execution. This allows the server to process multiple requests concurrently, ensuring that one slow request doesn't hold up the others. It's like having a team of chefs in a busy kitchen, each preparing a dish independently, ensuring that all orders are fulfilled promptly.

Building a Concurrent Web Server in Go

Here's an example of a concurrent web server in Go

Code snippet

```
package main

import (

 "fmt"

 "net/http"

 "sync"

)


var counter int

var mutex sync.Mutex


func handler(w http.ResponseWriter, r
*http.Request) {

 mutex.Lock()

 counter++

 mutex.Unlock()
```

```go
    fmt.Fprintf(w, "Hello, you've requested: %s\n",
r.URL.Path)

    fmt.Fprintf(w, "Total requests served: %d\n",
counter)

}



func main() {

  http.HandleFunc("/", handler) // Register the
handler function for all paths



  server := &http.Server{

    Addr: ":8080", // Configure the server to
listen on port 8080

  }



  fmt.Println("Starting server on:8080...")

  go func() {

    err := server.ListenAndServe() // Start the
server in a new goroutine

    if err != nil {

      fmt.Println("Error starting server:",
err.Error())

    }
```

```
} ()
```

```
// Keep the program running
```

```
select {}
```

```
}
```

In this example, we define a handler function that simply writes a greeting message and a counter to the response. The http.HandleFunc function registers this handler for all incoming requests.

The key to concurrency lies in how we start the server. We create a new goroutine using go func() {... }() and call server.ListenAndServe() within that goroutine. This allows the server to listen for and handle incoming requests concurrently without blocking the main program.

Benefits of this Approach

This concurrent web server offers several benefits

- Improved Responsiveness: Users experience faster response times as their requests are processed concurrently, even under heavy load.
- Increased Throughput: The server can handle a larger number of requests per unit of time, improving overall throughput and efficiency.
- Enhanced Scalability: The server can scale more effectively to handle increasing client demand, as it can utilize multiple processor cores and distribute the workload across multiple goroutines.

Real-World Applications

Concurrent web servers are the backbone of many popular websites and services. They enable these services to handle millions of users simultaneously, providing a smooth and responsive experience.

Examples include

- E-commerce websites: During peak shopping seasons, e-commerce websites need to handle a massive influx of traffic and orders. Concurrent web servers ensure that the website remains responsive and can process orders efficiently.
- Social media platforms: Social media platforms like Twitter and Facebook handle millions of concurrent users posting updates, sharing content, and interacting with each other. Concurrency is essential for maintaining a real-time and engaging user experience.
- Streaming services: Streaming services like Netflix and Spotify need to handle a large number of users streaming videos and music concurrently. Concurrent web servers ensure smooth playback and prevent buffering issues.

By understanding and applying the principles of concurrency in Go, you can build high-performance web servers that can handle the demands of the modern internet and provide a seamless experience for your users.

Chapter 7: Building RESTful APIs

In today's interconnected world, APIs (Application Programming Interfaces) are the connective tissue that allows different applications to communicate and share data. They are the unsung heroes behind many of the services we use every day, enabling seamless integration and data exchange between different systems. And when it comes to building APIs, the RESTful architectural style has emerged as the dominant approach, providing a standardized and flexible way to design and interact with web services.

In this chapter, we'll explore the world of RESTful APIs in Go. We'll delve into the core principles of REST, discuss best practices for designing APIs, and learn how to handle routing, requests, and responses using Go's net/http package. We'll also touch upon middleware, authentication, and the importance of API documentation.

7.1 RESTful Principles

Let's explore the world of RESTful APIs, a powerful architectural style that has revolutionized how we build and interact with web services. REST, or Representational State Transfer, provides a set of guidelines and constraints for designing networked applications that are scalable, flexible, and easy to use.

Think of REST as a set of best practices for creating web services that are predictable, reliable, and interoperable. It's like a common language that different applications can speak to understand each other, regardless of their underlying technology or programming language.

The Core Tenets of REST

At the heart of REST are a few core principles that guide its design and implementation

- Client-Server Architecture: REST emphasizes a clear separation of concerns between the client and the server. The client, which could be a web browser, a mobile app, or another server, is responsible for the user interface and user experience. The server, on the other hand, is responsible for storing and managing data, processing requests, and enforcing business logic. This separation allows for independent evolution and scalability of both the client and the server.
- Statelessness: In a RESTful architecture, each request from the client to the server must contain all the information necessary for the server to understand and process the request. The server does[1] not store any client context between requests. This makes RESTful APIs highly scalable, as the server doesn't need to maintain any client-specific state. It's like a vending machine: you insert your coins and make your selection, and the machine dispenses your item without remembering your previous purchases.
- Cacheability: RESTful APIs encourage the use of caching to improve performance and scalability. Responses from the server should explicitly state whether they can be cached or not, allowing clients to store responses and reuse them for subsequent requests, reducing the load on the server.
- Uniform Interface: RESTful APIs utilize a uniform interface for interacting with resources. This interface is based on the standard HTTP methods: GET for retrieving data, POST for creating data, PUT for updating data, and DELETE for deleting data. This consistent use of HTTP methods makes RESTful APIs predictable and easy to understand.

- Layered System: REST allows for a layered system architecture, where the client interacts with the server through one or more intermediary layers. These layers might include load balancers, security filters, or caching layers. This allows for flexibility and scalability, as you can add or remove layers without affecting the client or the server.
- Code on Demand (Optional): RESTful APIs can optionally provide code on demand to extend or customize the functionality of the client. This might involve sending JavaScript code to the client to perform client-side validation or to enhance the user interface.

Benefits of RESTful APIs

RESTful APIs offer several benefits

- Scalability: The stateless nature of REST makes it easy to scale APIs to handle a large number of clients and requests.
- Flexibility: RESTful APIs can be used with various data formats, such as JSON or XML, and can be accessed from different types of clients, such as web browsers, mobile apps, or other servers.
- Interoperability: The use of standard HTTP methods and URLs makes RESTful APIs highly interoperable, allowing different systems to communicate seamlessly.
- Ease of Use: The consistent and predictable nature of RESTful APIs makes them easy to understand and use for developers.
- Evolution: RESTful APIs can evolve over time without breaking existing clients, as long as the interface remains consistent.

Real-World Examples

RESTful APIs are ubiquitous in the modern web. Here are a few examples

- Social Media APIs: Social media platforms like Twitter and Facebook provide RESTful APIs that allow developers to access and interact with their data, such as user profiles, posts, and comments.
- E-commerce APIs: E-commerce platforms like Amazon and eBay offer RESTful APIs that allow developers to build applications that interact with their product catalogs, shopping carts, and order management systems.
- Cloud APIs: Cloud providers like AWS and Google Cloud offer RESTful APIs for managing cloud resources, such as virtual machines, storage, and databases.
- Payment Gateways: Payment gateways like Stripe and PayPal provide RESTful APIs for processing online payments.

By understanding and applying the principles of REST, you can design and build APIs that are scalable, flexible, and easy to use, enabling seamless integration and data exchange between different applications and systems.

7.2 Designing APIs

Designing APIs is a bit like being an architect. You're not just building a functional structure; you're crafting an interface that others will interact with. A well-designed API is like a well-designed building: intuitive, easy to navigate, and aesthetically pleasing. In the world of software, this translates to APIs that are clear, consistent, and easy to use for developers.

Let's explore some best practices for designing RESTful APIs that are both functional and developer-friendly

Use Nouns for Resources

When defining the endpoints in your API, focus on using nouns to represent resources. Think of resources as the "things" your API provides access to. These could be users, products, orders, or any other entities relevant to your application.

For example, instead of using an endpoint like /getUser, use /users to represent the collection of users. This noun-based approach makes your API more intuitive and predictable.

Use HTTP Methods Appropriately

RESTful APIs leverage the standard HTTP methods (GET, POST, PUT, DELETE) to perform actions on resources.

Use these methods consistently and according to their intended purpose

- GET: Retrieve data. Use GET requests to fetch information about a resource or a collection of resources. For example, GET /users to retrieve all users or GET /users/123 to retrieve a specific user with ID 123.
- POST: Create data. Use POST requests to create new resources. For example, POST /users to create a new user.
- PUT: Update data. Use PUT requests to update an existing resource. For example, PUT /users/123 to update the user with ID 123.
- DELETE: Delete data. Use DELETE requests to delete a resource. For example, DELETE /users/123 to delete the user with ID 123.

Keep it Consistent

Consistency is key in API design. Use consistent naming conventions for your resources and endpoints. If you use camelCase for one endpoint, stick with it throughout your API. Similarly, maintain consistency in your data formats (e.g., JSON) and error handling practices.

Versioning

As your API evolves, you'll inevitably need to make changes. To avoid breaking existing clients that rely on your API, introduce versioning in your API URLs. This allows you to maintain backward compatibility while providing newer versions with additional features or changes.

For example, you could use /v1/users for the initial version of your user API and /v2/users for a newer version with updated functionality.

Error Handling

Errors are a fact of life in software development, and your API should be prepared to handle them gracefully. Provide informative error messages in your responses, and use appropriate HTTP status codes to indicate the type of error that occurred.

For example, if a client requests a resource that doesn't exist, return a 404 Not Found status code with a message indicating that the resource was not found.

Documentation

Documentation is crucial for any API. It's the guidebook that helps developers understand and use your API effectively.

Good API documentation should be

- Comprehensive: Cover all aspects of your API, including resources, methods, parameters, responses, and error handling.
- Clear and Concise: Use simple language and avoid jargon.
- Well-Structured: Organize the documentation in a logical and easy-to-navigate manner.
- Up-to-Date: Keep the documentation current with any changes or updates to your API.

Consider using tools like Swagger or OpenAPI to generate interactive documentation that allows developers to explore and test your API directly.

Real-World Examples

Many successful APIs exemplify these best practices

- Stripe API: Stripe, a popular payment gateway, provides a well-designed and documented API that is widely praised by developers for its ease of use and consistency.
- Twilio API: Twilio, a communication platform, offers a comprehensive API with clear documentation and consistent naming conventions.
- GitHub API: GitHub's API is well-structured, versioned, and provides detailed documentation with examples and use cases.

By following these best practices, you can design APIs that are not only functional and efficient but also a pleasure to work with for developers. Remember, a well-designed API is an investment in your users, making it easier for them to integrate with your services and build innovative applications on top of your platform.

7.3 Routing and Request Handling in Go

Now that we've explored the principles of RESTful API design, let's dive into the practical aspects of building APIs in Go. Go's net/http package provides a robust and flexible framework for handling HTTP requests and routing them to the appropriate handlers. Think of it as the traffic controller of your API, directing incoming requests to the right destinations.

Routing

Routing is the process of mapping incoming HTTP requests to specific handler functions based on the request's URL path and method. It's like having a receptionist who directs calls to the appropriate departments based on the caller's request.

In Go, the http.HandleFunc function is the primary tool for routing requests. It takes two arguments

- pattern: A string pattern that matches the URL path of the request. This pattern can include wildcards and variables to match different types of requests.
- handler: The handler function that will be called to process the request if the pattern matches.

Here's a simple example

Code snippet

```
http.HandleFunc("/", homeHandler) // Handle
requests to the root path ("/")

http.HandleFunc("/users", usersHandler) // Handle
requests to "/users"
```

This code registers two handler functions: homeHandler for requests to the root path and usersHandler for requests to the /users path.

Request Handling

Handler functions are the heart of your API. They are responsible for processing incoming requests, performing any necessary logic, and generating the appropriate responses. Think of them as the workers in your API factory, each specialized in handling a specific type of request.

Handler functions in Go typically take two arguments

- http.ResponseWriter: This interface provides methods for writing the response back to the client, including setting headers, writing the response body, and setting the status code.
- http.Request: This struct contains information about the incoming request, including the request method, URL, headers, and body.

Here's an example of a simple handler function

```
Code snippet

func helloHandler(w http.ResponseWriter, r
*http.Request) {

    fmt.Fprintf(w, "Hello, you've requested:
%s\n", r.URL.Path)

}
```

This handler function simply writes a greeting message to the response, including the requested URL path.

Handling Different HTTP Methods

RESTful APIs utilize different HTTP methods for different actions on resources. You can check the request method in your handler functions using the r.Method field.

Here's an example of a handler that handles both GET and POST requests

Code snippet

```
func usersHandler(w http.ResponseWriter, r
*http.Request) {

    if r.Method == http.MethodGet {

        // Handle GET request (e.g., retrieve
users)

    } else if r.Method == http.MethodPost {

        // Handle POST request (e.g., create a
new user)

    } else {

        http.Error(w, "Invalid request method",
http.StatusMethodNotAllowed)

    }

}
```

Extracting Data from Requests

You can extract data from incoming requests using various methods

- URL Parameters: For requests like /users/123, you can extract the user ID (123) from the URL path.
- Query Parameters: For requests like /users?name=john, you can extract the name parameter from the query string.
- Request Body: For POST or PUT requests, you can extract data from the request body, which might be in JSON, XML, or other formats.

Generating Responses

The http.ResponseWriter interface provides methods for generating responses

- WriteHeader: Sets the HTTP status code of the response.
- Write: Writes data to the response body.
- Header: Provides access to the response headers, allowing you to set cookies or other headers.

Example: A Simple RESTful API

Let's build a simple RESTful API for managing a list of books

```
Code snippet

package main


import (
```

```go
    "encoding/json"

    "fmt"

    "net/http"

)


type Book struct {

  Title   string `json:"title"`

  Author  string `json:"author"`

}


var booksBook


func getBooks(w http.ResponseWriter, r
*http.Request) {

  json.NewEncoder(w).Encode(books)

}


func createBook(w http.ResponseWriter, r
*http.Request) {

  var newBook Book

  json.NewDecoder(r.Body).Decode(&newBook)
```

```go
    books = append(books, newBook)

    w.WriteHeader(http.StatusCreated)

    json.NewEncoder(w).Encode(newBook)

}


func main() {

  http.HandleFunc("/books", func(w
http.ResponseWriter, r *http.Request) {

    if r.Method == http.MethodGet {

      getBooks(w, r)

    } else if r.Method == http.MethodPost {

      createBook(w, r)

    } else {

      http.Error(w, "Invalid request method",
http.StatusMethodNotAllowed)

    }

  })


  fmt.Println("Starting server on:8080...")

  http.ListenAndServe(":8080", nil)

}
```

This API provides two endpoints

- GET /books: Retrieves all books.
- POST /books: Creates a new book.

By understanding routing and request handling in Go, you can build robust and flexible RESTful APIs that provide valuable services and data to your users. Remember, good routing and request handling are essential for creating APIs that are efficient, reliable, and easy to use.

7.4 Middleware and Authentication

Middleware and authentication are essential components of building secure and robust RESTful APIs. Middleware acts like a gatekeeper, intercepting requests and performing actions before or after they reach your main handler functions. Authentication verifies the identity of clients, ensuring that only authorized users can access your API's resources.

Think of middleware as a series of checkpoints that a request passes through before reaching its final destination. Each checkpoint can perform a specific task, such as logging the request, checking for authentication credentials, or modifying the request or response.

Authentication, on the other hand, is like the bouncer at the door, checking IDs to ensure that only those with the right credentials are allowed in. It's a crucial security measure that protects your API from unauthorized access and potential misuse.

Middleware in Go

In Go, middleware is typically implemented as functions that take a handler function as input and return a new handler function that wraps around the original handler. This allows you to chain multiple middleware functions together, creating a pipeline of actions that are executed before or after the main handler.

Here's a simple example of a middleware function that logs the request method and URL

```
Code snippet

func loggingMiddleware(next http.Handler)
http.Handler {

    return http.HandlerFunc(func(w
http.ResponseWriter, r *http.Request) {

        fmt.Printf("Received %s request for
%s\n", r.Method, r.URL.Path)

        next.ServeHTTP(w, r) // Call the next
handler in the chain

    })

}
```

This middleware function takes a http.Handler as input and returns a new http.Handler that logs the request information before calling the original handler using next.ServeHTTP(w, r).

Authentication

Authentication is the process of verifying the identity of a client making a request to your API.

There are various authentication mechanisms, including

- API Keys: Clients are assigned unique API keys that they include in their requests, typically as a header or query parameter. The server can then verify the API key to authenticate the client.

- Basic Authentication: Clients send their username and password in the Authorization header, encoded using Base64.
- Bearer Tokens (JWTs): Clients send a JSON Web Token (JWT) in the Authorization header. The server can verify the token's signature and extract information about the user from the token.
- OAuth 2.0: A more complex authorization framework that allows clients to delegate access to their resources to third-party applications without sharing their credentials.

Implementing Authentication in Go

You can implement authentication in your Go APIs using middleware functions. The middleware can intercept requests, check for authentication credentials, and either allow or deny access to the API based on the authentication status.

Here's an example of a middleware function that checks for an API key in the request header

Code snippet

```
func authMiddleware(next http.Handler)
http.Handler {

    return http.HandlerFunc(func(w
http.ResponseWriter, r *http.Request) {

        apiKey:= r.Header.Get("X-API-Key")

        if apiKey == "" || apiKey!=
"your_api_key" {

            http.Error(w, "Unauthorized",
http.StatusUnauthorized)
```

```
        return

    }



        next.ServeHTTP(w, r) // Call the next
handler if authenticated

    })

}
```

This middleware function checks for the X-API-Key header in the request. If the header is missing or the API key is invalid, it returns a 401 Unauthorized error. Otherwise, it allows the request to proceed to the next handler.

Combining Middleware

You can chain multiple middleware functions together to create a pipeline of actions. For example, you might use one middleware function for logging, another for authentication, and a third for authorization.

```
Code snippet

http.Handle("/users",
authMiddleware(loggingMiddleware(http.HandlerFunc
(usersHandler))))
```

In this example, the usersHandler is wrapped with the loggingMiddleware and then the authMiddleware. This means that the logging middleware will be executed first, followed by the authentication middleware, and finally the usersHandler.

Real-World Examples

Middleware and authentication are used extensively in real-world APIs

- E-commerce APIs: Authentication is used to protect user accounts and prevent unauthorized access to sensitive data like payment information.
- Social Media APIs: Middleware is used to rate-limit requests, preventing abuse and ensuring fair access to the API for all users.
- Cloud APIs: Authentication and authorization are used to control access to cloud resources, ensuring that only authorized users can perform actions like creating or deleting virtual machines.

By understanding and applying middleware and authentication techniques in your Go APIs, you can build secure and robust services that protect your data and provide a safe and reliable experience for your users.

7.5 API Documentation

Imagine you've stumbled upon a fascinating new tool, but there's no manual, no instructions, and no one to guide you. Frustrating, right? That's exactly how developers feel when they encounter an API without proper documentation. API documentation is the instruction manual for your API, the guidebook that helps developers understand how to use your API effectively.

Good API documentation is essential for the success of your API. It empowers developers to integrate your API into their applications smoothly, reducing frustration and increasing adoption. Think of it as the bridge that connects your API with the developers who will be using it.

What Makes Good API Documentation?

Good API documentation is characterized by several key qualities

- Completeness: It should cover all aspects of your API, leaving no stone unturned. This includes detailed descriptions of each endpoint, the supported HTTP methods, request parameters, response formats, and possible error codes.
- Clarity and Conciseness: Use clear and concise language, avoiding jargon or technical terms that might confuse developers. Write as if you're explaining your API to a friend who is new to programming.
- Well-Structured: Organize the documentation in a logical and easy-to-navigate manner. Use headings, subheadings, and a table of contents to make it easy for developers to find the information they need.
- Up-to-Date: Keep the documentation current with any changes or updates to your API. Outdated documentation can lead to frustration and errors for developers.
- Examples: Provide plenty of examples to illustrate how to use your API. Include code snippets in various programming languages to show how to make requests and handle responses.
- Interactive Elements (Optional): Consider incorporating interactive elements, such as a console where developers can try out API calls directly within the documentation. This can significantly enhance the learning and exploration process.

Tools for Generating API Documentation

Thankfully, you don't have to write API documentation from scratch.

Several tools can help you generate professional and interactive documentation

- Swagger: A popular open-source framework for designing, building, and documenting RESTful APIs. Swagger provides a specification language (OpenAPI) for describing your API, and tools for generating interactive documentation from that specification.
- OpenAPI: The OpenAPI Specification (formerly Swagger Specification) is a standardized format for describing RESTful APIs. It allows you to define your API's endpoints, methods, parameters, responses, and other details in a machine-readable format.
- Postman: While primarily known as an API testing tool, Postman also allows you to generate documentation from your API requests and collections.
- Redoc: A tool that generates beautiful and interactive documentation from OpenAPI specifications.

Real-World Examples

Many successful APIs have excellent documentation that serves as a model for others

- Stripe API: Stripe's API documentation is widely praised for its clarity, completeness, and interactive elements. It includes code examples in various programming languages and a console for trying out API calls.

- Twilio API: Twilio's API documentation is well-structured and easy to navigate, with detailed descriptions of each endpoint and plenty of code examples.
- GitHub API: GitHub's API documentation is comprehensive and up-to-date, providing developers with everything they need to interact with GitHub programmatically.

Why API Documentation Matters

Good API documentation is an investment in the success of your API.

It provides numerous benefits

- Increased Adoption: Well-documented APIs are easier to understand and use, leading to increased adoption by developers.
- Reduced Support Costs: Clear documentation can help developers solve problems on their own, reducing the need for support requests.
- Improved Developer Experience: Good documentation makes it easier for developers to work with your API, leading to a more positive developer experience.
- Faster Integration: Clear and concise documentation can speed up the integration process, allowing developers to get up and running with your API quickly.

By prioritizing API documentation and utilizing the tools available, you can create a valuable resource for developers, making your API more accessible, user-friendly, and successful. Remember, good documentation is not just an afterthought; it's an integral part of the API development process.

Chapter 8: WebSockets

In the realm of web development, where real-time, bi-directional communication is becoming increasingly essential, WebSockets emerge as a powerful tool. Unlike traditional HTTP, which follows a request-response pattern, WebSockets provide a persistent connection between the client and the server, allowing for seamless, low-latency communication in both directions.

Think of WebSockets as a continuous conversation between two friends, where they can freely exchange messages without the formality of constantly asking and answering questions. This persistent connection opens up a world of possibilities for building interactive and engaging web applications.

In this chapter, we'll explore the world of WebSockets in Go. We'll start with an introduction to the WebSocket protocol, then delve into how to implement WebSockets in Go using the gorilla/websocket package. We'll also discuss how to handle real-time communication and explore various use cases for WebSockets.

8.1 Introduction to WebSockets

In the ever-evolving landscape of web development, where real-time interactivity and dynamic updates are becoming increasingly crucial, WebSockets have emerged as a game-changer. Unlike traditional HTTP communication, which follows a request-response paradigm, WebSockets provide a persistent, bi-directional communication channel between a client and a server.

Think of it like this: HTTP is like sending a letter. You write your message, put it in an envelope, address it, and send it off. Then, you wait for a reply. WebSockets, on the other hand, are like having a phone conversation. You establish a connection, and then you can freely exchange messages back and forth in real-time.

This persistent connection that WebSockets provide opens up a world of possibilities for building interactive and engaging web applications. It allows for seamless, low-latency communication, making it ideal for applications that require real-time updates, such as chat applications, online games, collaborative tools, and real-time dashboards.

Understanding the WebSocket Protocol

WebSockets are a communication protocol that provides a full-duplex, bi-directional communication channel over a single TCP connection. This means that both the client and the server can send and receive data simultaneously without the overhead of establishing new connections for each message. It's like having a dedicated two-way communication link, ensuring that messages can flow freely in both directions.

The WebSocket Handshake

The WebSocket connection begins with a handshake, a process where the client and server agree to upgrade their communication from a regular HTTP connection to a WebSocket connection. This handshake involves the client sending a request to the server with specific headers indicating its desire to switch protocols. The server, if it supports WebSockets, responds with an acceptance message, and the connection is upgraded.

Once the handshake is complete, the underlying TCP connection remains open, and both the client and the server can start exchanging data in the form of WebSocket frames.

WebSocket Frames

WebSocket communication is based on frames, which are small packets of data that carry information between the client and the server.

These frames can contain various types of data

- Text Data: Regular text messages, such as chat messages or code updates.
- Binary Data: Raw binary data, such as images, audio, or video streams.
- Control Frames: Special frames that carry control information, such as ping/pong frames for keep-alive signals or close frames to initiate the termination of the connection.

This framing mechanism allows for efficient and flexible data exchange, accommodating different types of content and control signals.

Advantages of WebSockets

WebSockets offer several advantages over traditional HTTP communication

- Real-time Communication: WebSockets enable true real-time communication, where data is exchanged and updated instantly, making them perfect for applications that require immediate feedback and updates.
- Bi-directional Communication: The full-duplex nature of WebSockets allows for seamless communication in both directions, enabling more interactive and dynamic applications.
- Low Latency: The persistent connection reduces latency, as there's no need to establish new connections for each

message, making WebSockets ideal for applications where responsiveness is crucial.

- Efficiency: The lightweight framing mechanism reduces overhead and improves efficiency, especially for applications that exchange frequent small messages.

Real-World Examples

WebSockets are used in a wide range of applications today

- Chat Applications: Popular chat applications like Slack, Discord, and Facebook Messenger use WebSockets to provide real-time messaging functionality.
- Online Games: Online multiplayer games rely on WebSockets to enable real-time interaction between players, ensuring a smooth and responsive gaming experience.
- Collaborative Tools: Collaborative editing tools like Google Docs use WebSockets to allow multiple users to edit the same document simultaneously and see each other's changes in real-time.
- Financial Trading Platforms: Real-time trading platforms use WebSockets to stream live market data and execute trades with low latency.
- IoT Applications: WebSockets can be used to communicate with Internet of Things (IoT) devices, enabling real-time monitoring and control of smart home devices, industrial sensors, and other connected devices.

By understanding the WebSocket protocol and its capabilities, you can leverage its power to build highly interactive and engaging web applications that provide a seamless and real-time user experience.

8.2 Implementing WebSockets in Go

While Go's standard library provides excellent support for various network protocols, it doesn't include explicit features for working with WebSockets. However, the vibrant Go ecosystem comes to the rescue with the gorilla/websocket package. This popular third-party package offers a robust and well-tested implementation of the WebSocket protocol, making it a breeze to integrate WebSockets into your Go applications.

Think of the gorilla/websocket package as a specialized toolkit for building WebSocket-based applications in Go. It provides the necessary functions and data structures for handling WebSocket handshakes, reading and writing messages, and managing connections, abstracting away the low-level details and allowing you to focus on the core logic of your application.

Installing the gorilla/websocket Package

Before we embark on our WebSocket journey, let's ensure you have the gorilla/websocket package installed. You can easily add it to your project using the following command in your terminal:

Bash

```
go get github.com/gorilla/websocket
```

This command will fetch the package from its online repository and install it in your Go workspace, making it ready for use in your code.

Upgrading to a WebSocket Connection

The first step in implementing WebSockets is to upgrade an existing HTTP connection to a WebSocket connection. This is where the gorilla/websocket package shines. It provides an Upgrader type that handles the WebSocket handshake process, taking care of the protocol switching and establishing the persistent connection.

Think of the Upgrader as the diplomat that negotiates the transition from a regular HTTP connection to a WebSocket connection. It takes care of the necessary communication with the client, ensuring a smooth and seamless upgrade.

Here's how you typically set up the Upgrader

Code snippet

```
var upgrader = websocket.Upgrader{

    ReadBufferSize:  1024,

    WriteBufferSize: 1024,

    // You can add more options here, such as
checking the origin of the request

}
```

This code creates an Upgrader with default read and write buffer sizes of 1024 bytes each. You can customize these buffer sizes if needed, or add additional options, such as checking the origin of the request to prevent cross-site WebSocket hijacking attacks, a security measure that ensures that only authorized clients can establish WebSocket connections.

To perform the actual upgrade, you'll use the Upgrade() method of the Upgrader in your HTTP handler function

Code snippet

```
func handler(w http.ResponseWriter, r
*http.Request) {
```

```
conn, err:= upgrader.Upgrade(w, r, nil)

if err!= nil {

    log.Println(err)

    return

}

defer conn.Close()



//... handle the WebSocket connection...

}
```

This code snippet attempts to upgrade the incoming HTTP connection to a WebSocket connection using the upgrader.Upgrade() method. If the upgrade is successful, it returns a *websocket.Conn object, which represents the established WebSocket connection. If there's an error during the upgrade process, it's important to handle it gracefully, as shown in the example, by logging the error and returning from the handler.

Reading and Writing Messages

Once the WebSocket connection is established, the real-time communication begins. The gorilla/websocket package provides convenient methods for reading and writing messages between the client and the server:

- ReadMessage(): This method reads a message from the WebSocket connection. It returns the type of the message (text or binary) and the message payload as a byte slice. Think of it as receiving a message through the WebSocket pipe.

- WriteMessage(): This method writes a message to the WebSocket connection. It takes the message type and the message payload as arguments. Think of it as sending a message through the WebSocket pipe.

Here's an example of how to use these methods to echo messages back to the client

```
Code snippet

//... inside the handler function...


for {
    // Read message from the client

    messageType, p, err:= conn.ReadMessage()

    if err!= nil {

        log.Println(err)

        return

    }


    // Process the message (e.g., print it to the console)

    fmt.Printf("Received: %s\n", string(p))


    // Send a response back to the client
```

```
    if err:= conn.WriteMessage(messageType, p);
err!= nil {

        log.Println(err)

        return

    }

}
```

This code snippet continuously reads messages from the client using conn.ReadMessage(), processes them (in this case, simply printing them to the console), and then sends the same message back to the client using conn.WriteMessage(). This creates a simple echo server where the client receives back whatever it sends.

Handling Connection Closure

WebSocket connections, like any other network connections, can be closed by either the client or the server. The gorilla/websocket package provides ways to detect and handle connection closures gracefully:

- Close(): This method closes the WebSocket connection from the server-side. It's like hanging up the phone.
- NextReader(): This method returns an error if the connection is closed by the client. It's like noticing that the other party has hung up.

You can use these methods to gracefully handle connection closures and perform any necessary cleanup tasks, such as releasing resources or notifying other parts of your application.

Example

Let's put these concepts together and build a simple chat server that allows multiple clients to connect and exchange messages in real-time:

Code snippet

```
package main


import (

  "fmt"

  "log"

  "net/http"


  "github.com/gorilla/websocket"

)



var upgrader = websocket.Upgrader{} // Use
default options



// A hub to manage connected clients

type Hub struct {

  clients     map[*websocket.Conn]bool

  broadcast   chanbyte
```

```go
    register    chan *websocket.Conn

    unregister chan *websocket.Conn

}


func newHub() *Hub {

  return &Hub{

    broadcast:  make(chanbyte),

    register:   make(chan *websocket.Conn),

    unregister: make(chan *websocket.Conn),

    clients:    make(map[*websocket.Conn]bool),

  }

}


func (h *Hub) run() {

  for {

    select {

    case client:= <-h.register:

      h.clients[client] = true

    case client:= <-h.unregister:

      if _, ok:= h.clients[client]; ok {
```

```go
        delete(h.clients, client)

        close(client.Close)

      }

    case message:= <-h.broadcast:

      for client:= range h.clients {

        err:=
client.WriteMessage(websocket.TextMessage,
message)

        if err!= nil {

          log.Printf("Error writing message to client:
%v", err)

          // Handle the error (e.g., close the
connection)

        }

      }

    }

  }

}


var hub = newHub()


func chatHandler(w http.ResponseWriter, r
*http.Request) {
```

```go
conn, err:= upgrader.Upgrade(w, r, nil)

if err!= nil {

  log.Println(err)

  return

}

defer conn.Close()


hub.register <- conn // Register the client with
the hub


for {

  // Read message from browser

  _, msg, err:= conn.ReadMessage()

  if err!= nil {

    if websocket.IsUnexpectedCloseError(err,
websocket.CloseGoingAway,
websocket.CloseAbnormalClosure) {

      log.Printf("Error reading message: %v", err)

    }

    hub.unregister <- conn // Unregister the
client

    break
```

```
    }


    hub.broadcast <- msg // Broadcast the message
to all clients

  }

}



func main() {

  go hub.run() // Start the hub in a new goroutine



  fmt.Println("Starting WebSocket chat server
on:8080...")

  http.HandleFunc("/chat", chatHandler)

  http.ListenAndServe(":8080", nil)

}
```

This chat server demonstrates a more complex use case of WebSockets. It uses a Hub to manage connected clients and broadcast messages to all clients. Each client connection is handled in a separate goroutine, and channels are used to communicate between the clients and the hub.

By utilizing the gorilla/websocket package and applying the principles of concurrency, you can build sophisticated WebSocket-based applications in Go, enabling real-time communication and interactivity for a wide range of use cases.

8.3 Handling Real-time Communication

WebSockets unlock the potential for truly real-time communication on the web, where data flows seamlessly between clients and servers, creating dynamic and interactive experiences. It's like having a live conversation, where you can respond and react to messages instantly, without the delays of traditional request-response cycles.

This real-time capability opens up a world of possibilities for web applications. Imagine building a chat application where messages appear instantly, a collaborative document editor where you can see others' changes as they type, or a real-time dashboard that updates with live data. WebSockets make all of this possible.

The Essence of Real-time Communication

Real-time communication is characterized by low latency and high frequency updates. It's about delivering information as quickly as possible, minimizing the delay between an event happening and the user being notified. This immediacy is what creates the feeling of a "live" and interactive experience.

WebSockets are perfectly suited for this task. Their persistent connection and bi-directional communication capabilities allow for seamless and efficient data exchange, making them the ideal choice for real-time applications.

Building Blocks of Real-time Communication with WebSockets

Let's break down the key components of handling real-time communication with WebSockets

- Connection Management: Establishing and maintaining WebSocket connections is the foundation of real-time communication. The gorilla/websocket package, as we discussed earlier, provides the tools for handling the WebSocket handshake and managing the connection lifecycle.

- Message Handling: Once the connection is established, the focus shifts to handling messages. This involves reading incoming messages from the client, processing them, and sending responses or updates back to the client or other connected clients.
- Concurrency: Real-time applications often need to handle multiple connections and messages concurrently. Go's concurrency primitives, goroutines and channels, are instrumental in managing this concurrency effectively.
- Data Serialization: The data exchanged over WebSockets needs to be serialized into a format that both the client and the server can understand. JSON is a popular choice for its simplicity and wide support, but other formats like MessagePack or Protobuf can also be used depending on the application's needs.

Example

Let's illustrate these concepts with a more elaborate example of a real-time chat application

```
Code snippet

package main


import (

  "fmt"

  "log"
```

```go
	"net/http"

	"github.com/gorilla/websocket"
)


var upgrader = websocket.Upgrader{} // Use
default options


// Client represents a connected chat user

type Client struct {

	conn *websocket.Conn

	send chanbyte

}


// Hub manages connected clients and broadcasts
messages

type Hub struct {

	clients    map[*Client]bool

	broadcast  chanbyte

	register   chan *Client

	unregister chan *Client
```

```go
}

func newHub() *Hub {
  return &Hub{
    broadcast:  make(chanbyte),
    register:   make(chan *Client),
    unregister: make(chan *Client),
    clients:    make(map[*Client]bool),
  }
}


func (h *Hub) run() {
  for {
    select {
    case client:= <-h.register:
      h.clients[client] = true
    case client:= <-h.unregister:
      if _, ok:= h.clients[client]; ok {
        delete(h.clients, client)
        close(client.send)
```

```go
    }
  case message:= <-h.broadcast:
    for client:= range h.clients {
      select {
      case client.send <- message:
      default:
        close(client.send)
        delete(h.clients, client)
      }
    }
    }
  }
}


var hub = newHub()


func chatHandler(w http.ResponseWriter, r
*http.Request) {
  conn, err:= upgrader.Upgrade(w, r, nil)
  if err!= nil {
    log.Println(err)
```

```go
    return
  }

  defer conn.Close()


  client:= &Client{conn: conn, send:
make(chanbyte, 256)}
  hub.register <- client


  go client.writePump()

  go client.readPump()
}


func (c *Client) readPump() {
  defer func() {
    hub.unregister <- c

    c.conn.Close()
  }()
  c.conn.SetReadLimit(512)
  for {
    _, message, err:= c.conn.ReadMessage()
    if err!= nil {
```

```go
    if websocket.IsUnexpectedCloseError(err,
websocket.CloseGoingAway,
websocket.CloseAbnormalClosure) {

        log.Printf("Error reading message: %v", err)

    }

    break

    }

    hub.broadcast <- message

    }

}


func (c *Client) writePump() {
    defer func() {

        c.conn.Close()

    }()

    for {

        select {

        case message, ok:= <-c.send:

            if!ok {


c.conn.WriteMessage(websocket.CloseMessage,byte{}
)
```

```
        return

    }

    c.conn.WriteMessage(websocket.TextMessage,
message)

    }

  }

}


func main() {

  go hub.run() // Start the hub in a new goroutine


  fmt.Println("Starting WebSocket chat server
on:8080...")

  http.HandleFunc("/chat", chatHandler)

  http.ListenAndServe(":8080", nil)

}
```

In this example

- We define a Client struct to represent each connected client, with a WebSocket connection and a channel for sending messages.
- The Hub manages connected clients, broadcasts messages, and handles client registration and unregistration.

- The chatHandler function upgrades the HTTP connection to a WebSocket connection, creates a new Client, and registers it with the hub.
- The readPump function reads messages from the client and broadcasts them to the hub.
- The writePump function sends messages from the hub to the client.

This example demonstrates how to handle real-time communication using WebSockets in Go. It showcases the use of goroutines and channels to manage concurrency and ensure efficient message delivery.

Key Considerations for Real-time Communication

When building real-time applications with WebSockets, keep these considerations in mind

- Error Handling: Network connections can be unreliable, so implement robust error handling to gracefully handle disconnections and other errors.
- Scalability: Design your application to handle a large number of concurrent connections and messages efficiently.
- Security: Protect your WebSocket endpoints from unauthorized access and potential vulnerabilities.
- Performance: Optimize your code to minimize latency and ensure smooth real-time updates.

By mastering the techniques of handling real-time communication with WebSockets in Go, you can build dynamic and interactive web applications that provide a seamless and engaging experience for your users.

8.4 Use Cases for WebSockets

WebSockets have revolutionized the way we build interactive and real-time web applications. Their ability to provide a persistent, bi-directional communication channel between clients and servers opens up a world of possibilities for creating dynamic and engaging user experiences.

Let's explore some compelling use cases where WebSockets shine

Chat Applications

WebSockets are a natural fit for building chat applications, enabling real-time messaging between users. Whether it's a one-on-one chat, a group chat, or a chat room with thousands of users, WebSockets can handle the high volume of messages and deliver them instantly, creating a seamless and engaging chat experience.

Popular chat applications like Slack, Discord, and Facebook Messenger rely heavily on WebSockets to provide their real-time messaging capabilities.

Online Games

Online games, especially multiplayer games, require real-time interaction between players and the game server. WebSockets provide the low-latency communication necessary for a smooth and responsive gaming experience. They allow players to send commands, receive updates on game state, and interact with other players in real-time, creating an immersive and engaging gaming environment.

Popular online games like Agar.io and Slither.io utilize WebSockets to handle the real-time communication between players and the game server.

Collaborative Tools

WebSockets are transforming the way we collaborate online. They enable the creation of collaborative tools where multiple users can work together on the same document, project, or task in real-time. Changes made by one user are instantly reflected on the screens of other users, fostering a sense of shared presence and enabling seamless collaboration.

Google Docs, a popular collaborative document editing tool, uses WebSockets to allow multiple users to edit the same document simultaneously and see each other's changes in real-time.

Real-time Dashboards and Monitoring

WebSockets are ideal for building real-time dashboards and monitoring applications. They allow you to stream live data updates to clients, providing a dynamic and up-to-the-minute view of critical information. This can be used to monitor server performance, track financial markets, display social media feeds, or visualize sensor data from IoT devices.

Trading platforms, network monitoring tools, and social media analytics dashboards often utilize WebSockets to provide real-time updates and insights.

Financial Trading Platforms

In the fast-paced world of financial trading, every millisecond counts. WebSockets provide the low-latency communication necessary for traders to receive real-time market data, execute trades quickly, and stay ahead of the curve. They enable the creation of responsive and efficient trading platforms that can handle high volumes of data and transactions.

Online Education and Training

WebSockets can enhance online education and training platforms by enabling real-time interaction between instructors and students. They allow for features like live Q&A sessions, interactive quizzes, and collaborative exercises, creating a more engaging and effective learning environment.

Customer Support and Live Chat

WebSockets can power real-time customer support and live chat features on websites and web applications. They allow customers to connect with support agents instantly, receive immediate assistance, and resolve issues quickly, improving customer satisfaction and loyalty.

Internet of Things (IoT) Applications

WebSockets are increasingly used in IoT applications to enable real-time communication between connected devices and web applications. They allow for remote monitoring and control of smart home devices, industrial sensors, and other IoT devices, creating a more connected and automated world.

Beyond the Usual

The versatility of WebSockets extends beyond these common use cases. They can be used in various other scenarios where real-time communication and interactivity are desired:

- Real-time notifications: Deliver instant notifications to users, such as social media updates, news alerts, or system notifications.
- Live streaming: Stream live video or audio content, such as sports events, conferences, or online courses.

- Multi-user applications: Build applications where multiple users can interact with each other in real-time, such as collaborative whiteboards or online drawing tools.

By understanding the diverse applications of WebSockets, you can leverage their power to build innovative and engaging web experiences that cater to a wide range of user needs and scenarios.

Chapter 9: Network Security

In the vast and interconnected world of the internet, security is paramount. When building network applications, it's not enough to just ensure that data flows smoothly between clients and servers; we must also safeguard that data and protect our systems from malicious actors. Think of network security as the lock on your door, the shield that protects your valuable possessions from intruders.

In this chapter, we'll explore the essential aspects of network security in the context of Go programming. We'll delve into TLS/SSL encryption, discuss authentication and authorization mechanisms, examine common network vulnerabilities, and highlight security best practices to help you build secure and resilient network applications.

9.1 TLS/SSL Encryption

In today's hyper-connected world, where data traverses vast networks, security isn't just an option; it's a necessity. Imagine sending a confidential letter through the mail without an envelope. Anyone who handles that letter could potentially read its contents. That's essentially how data travels over the internet without encryption—exposed and vulnerable to prying eyes.

This is where TLS/SSL encryption comes in. It's like putting that sensitive letter in a secure, tamper-proof envelope, ensuring that only the intended recipient can read its contents. TLS (Transport Layer Security) and its predecessor SSL (Secure Sockets Layer) are cryptographic protocols that provide a secure communication channel over a network, protecting your data from eavesdropping, tampering, and other malicious activities.

Understanding the Mechanics of TLS/SSL

TLS/SSL employs a combination of cryptographic techniques to achieve its security goals

- Symmetric Encryption: This is like having a secret code that both you and your friend know. You use this code to scramble your message (encrypt it) before sending it, and your friend uses the same code to unscramble it (decrypt it) upon receiving it. In TLS/SSL, the client and the server establish a shared secret key, which is used for efficient encryption and decryption of the bulk of the data.
- Asymmetric Encryption: This is like having a special lockbox with two keys: a public key and a private key. You can give anyone the public key, but you keep the private key safe. Anyone can use the public key to lock something in the box, but only you, with the private key, can unlock it. In TLS/SSL, the server has a public key and a private key. The client uses the server's public key to encrypt a secret message (the shared key), and only the server, with its private key, can decrypt it. This ensures that the shared key is exchanged securely, even if someone is eavesdropping on the communication.
- Digital Certificates: How do you know that the public key you're using actually belongs to the server you intend to communicate with? That's where digital certificates come in. They are like digital passports, issued by trusted authorities, that verify the identity of the server. They contain the server's public key and other information, digitally signed by a Certificate Authority (CA). When a client connects to a server, the server presents its certificate, and the client can verify its authenticity using the CA's public key, which is typically pre-installed in the client's operating system or browser.

Implementing TLS/SSL in Go

Go's standard library provides excellent support for TLS/SSL through the crypto/tls package. This package offers the necessary tools for configuring and using TLS/SSL in your network applications.

To use TLS/SSL, you'll typically need

- A Digital Certificate: You can obtain a certificate from a trusted Certificate Authority (CA) like Let's Encrypt or Sectigo. For development and testing purposes, you can also generate a self-signed certificate.
- A TLS Configuration: This configuration specifies the certificate and key to use, along with other TLS parameters, such as the minimum TLS version to support or the cipher suites to use.

Here's an example of how to create a TLS listener in Go

Code snippet

```
package main


import (


"crypto/tls"


"fmt"


"log"
```

```go
    "net/http"


)


func handler(w http.ResponseWriter, r
*http.Request) {


  fmt.Fprintln(w, "Hello, secure world!")


}


func main() {


  // Load the certificate and key


  cert, err:=
tls.LoadX509KeyPair("server.crt",
"server.key")


  if err!= nil {


    log.Fatal(err)


  }


  // Create a TLS configuration
```

```go
tlsConfig:= &tls.Config{

  Certificates:tls.Certificate{cert},

  // You can add more configuration options
here, such as MinVersion or CipherSuites

  }

// Create a HTTPS server

server:= &http.Server{

  Addr:       ":443",

  TLSConfig: tlsConfig,

  Handler:    http.HandlerFunc(handler),

  }

  fmt.Println("Starting HTTPS server
on:443...")

  log.Fatal(server.ListenAndServeTLS("", ""))
// Start the server with TLS
```

```
}
```

In this example

1. We load the server's certificate and private key using tls.LoadX509KeyPair().
2. We create a tls.Config object, specifying the certificate to use.
3. We create an http.Server object, configuring it to use our TLS configuration.
4. We start the server using ListenAndServeTLS(), which listens for HTTPS connections on port 443.

Benefits of TLS/SSL

TLS/SSL provides several crucial security benefits

- Data Confidentiality: It encrypts the data exchanged between the client and the server, preventing eavesdropping and ensuring that only the intended recipient can read the data.
- Data Integrity: It ensures that the data is not tampered with during transmission. If an attacker modifies the data in transit, the recipient will be able to detect the tampering.
- Authentication: It verifies the identity of the server, ensuring that the client is communicating with the intended server and not an imposter. This prevents man-in-the-middle attacks, where an attacker intercepts the communication and impersonates the server.

By implementing TLS/SSL in your Go network applications, you provide a crucial layer of security, protecting your data and your users from potential threats. It's an essential step in building secure and trustworthy online services.

9.2 Authentication and Authorization

While encryption, like TLS/SSL, protects data in transit, authentication and authorization are the gatekeepers that control access to your application's resources. Think of authentication as verifying someone's identity, like checking their ID card, and authorization as determining what they're allowed to do once they're inside, like granting them access to specific rooms or areas.

In the context of network applications, authentication ensures that only legitimate users or clients can access your API or services, while authorization determines what actions they are permitted to perform once authenticated. This combination provides a crucial layer of security, preventing unauthorized access and potential misuse of your application.

Authentication Mechanisms

There are various authentication mechanisms you can employ in your Go network applications, each with its own strengths and weaknesses:

- API Keys: These are unique keys assigned to each client or user, allowing them to access your API. Clients typically include the API key in their requests, either as a header or a query parameter. The server can then validate the API key to authenticate the client. API keys are simple to implement but offer limited security if not handled carefully.
- Basic Authentication: This is a simple authentication scheme where the client sends their username and password in the Authorization header of the request, encoded using Base64. While easy to implement, Basic Authentication is considered less secure, especially if not

used over HTTPS, as the credentials are transmitted in plain text (though encoded).

- Bearer Tokens (JWTs): JSON Web Tokens (JWTs) are a more secure and flexible way to handle authentication. They are digitally signed tokens that contain information about the user, such as their ID or role. Clients include the JWT in the Authorization header of their requests. The server can then verify the token's signature and extract the user information to authenticate and authorize the request. JWTs are widely used in modern web applications due to their security and ease of use.

- OAuth 2.0: This is a more complex but powerful authorization framework that allows third-party applications to access user resources on your application without requiring the user to share their credentials with the third-party application. OAuth 2.0 is commonly used for social logins and integrations with other services.

Authorization

Once a user or client is authenticated, authorization comes into play. It determines what actions the authenticated user is allowed to perform. This can be based on various factors, such as the user's role, permissions, or the specific resource being accessed.

For example, in a blog application, an authenticated user might have permission to create and edit their own posts but not to delete other users' posts. Authorization ensures that users can only access and modify the resources they are authorized for.

Go Libraries for Authentication and Authorization

Go's ecosystem provides several libraries that can assist you with implementing authentication and authorization:

- jwt-go: This library provides functions for creating, signing, and verifying JWTs.
- oauth2: This library provides support for implementing OAuth 2.0 flows and handling tokens.
- casbin: This library provides a powerful authorization engine that supports various access control models, such as role-based access control (RBAC) and attribute-based access control (ABAC).

Implementing Authentication and Authorization in Go

You can implement authentication and authorization in your Go network applications using middleware functions. Middleware intercepts requests and can perform actions before or after the main handler function is executed.

Here's an example of a middleware function that checks for a JWT in the Authorization header

Code snippet

```
func authMiddleware(next http.Handler)
http.Handler {


    return http.HandlerFunc(func(w
http.ResponseWriter, r *http.Request) {


        tokenString :=
r.Header.Get("Authorization")


        if tokenString == "" {
```

```go
        http.Error(w, "Unauthorized",
http.StatusUnauthorized)


        return


    }



    // Parse and validate the JWT


    token, err:= jwt.Parse(tokenString,
func(token *jwt.Token) (interface{}, error)
{


        //... verify the token's
signature and claims...


    })




    if err!= nil ||!token.Valid {


        http.Error(w, "Unauthorized",
http.StatusUnauthorized)
```

```
            return




            // If the token is valid, extract
    user information and proceed


            //...




            next.ServeHTTP(w, r)


      })


  }
```

This middleware function extracts the JWT from the Authorization header, parses and validates it, and if the token is valid, extracts the user information and allows the request to proceed to the next handler.

Real-World Examples

Authentication and authorization are critical components of many real-world applications

- E-commerce Platforms: Authentication protects user accounts and prevents unauthorized access to sensitive information like payment details. Authorization ensures that users can only access and modify their own orders and information.
- Social Media Networks: Authentication verifies user identities and prevents fake accounts. Authorization controls what actions users can perform, such as posting content, following other users, or accessing private groups.
- Cloud Services: Authentication and authorization are used to control access to cloud resources, ensuring that only authorized users can perform actions like creating, modifying, or deleting virtual machines or storage buckets.

By implementing robust authentication and authorization mechanisms in your Go network applications, you can protect your users' data, prevent unauthorized access, and ensure the security and integrity of your services.

9.3 Common Network Vulnerabilities

Building secure network applications requires not only implementing security measures but also understanding the common vulnerabilities that attackers might exploit. Think of it like securing your home – you wouldn't just install a strong lock on the front door; you'd also check for other potential weaknesses, like open windows or weak spots in the fence.

In the world of network security, there's a wide range of vulnerabilities that can expose your application to attacks.

Let's explore some of the most common ones

Injection Attacks

Injection attacks occur when attackers inject malicious code into your application, often through user input fields or other external sources. This code can then be executed by your application, potentially compromising data, stealing information, or taking control of your systems.

- SQL Injection: This is a common attack where attackers inject malicious SQL code into database queries, potentially allowing them to access, modify, or delete data in your database. For example, if your application constructs SQL queries by concatenating user input directly into the query string, an attacker could inject malicious SQL code that modifies the query's behavior.
- Cross-Site Scripting (XSS): In XSS attacks, attackers inject malicious JavaScript code into web pages viewed by other users. This code can then steal user cookies, redirect users to malicious websites, or perform other harmful actions. For example, if your application displays user-generated content without proper sanitization, an attacker could inject JavaScript code that steals other users' session cookies.

Denial of Service (DoS) Attacks

Denial of Service attacks aim to disrupt the availability of your application or service, making it inaccessible to legitimate users. Attackers typically achieve this by flooding your server with a massive number of requests, overwhelming its resources and preventing it from responding to legitimate traffic.

- Distributed Denial of Service (DDoS): DDoS attacks are even more powerful, utilizing a network of compromised machines (botnets) to launch the attack, amplifying the volume of traffic and making it harder to defend against.

Man-in-the-Middle (MitM) Attacks

In MitM attacks, the attacker positions themselves between the client and the server, intercepting the communication and potentially stealing data, modifying it, or injecting malicious code. This can happen if the communication channel is not properly secured, such as when using HTTP instead of HTTPS.

- Session Hijacking: A type of MitM attack where the attacker steals the user's session cookie, allowing them to impersonate the user and access their account.

Cross-Site Request Forgery (CSRF) Attacks

CSRF attacks trick users into performing unwanted actions on your website. This typically happens when an attacker includes a malicious link or hidden form in a web page or email that, when clicked by a logged-in user, triggers an action on your website without the user's knowledge or consent.

For example, an attacker could send an email with a link that, when clicked, triggers a request to your application to transfer money from the user's account to the attacker's account. If the user is logged in to your application, the request might be executed without their knowledge.

Other Vulnerabilities

Besides these common vulnerabilities, there are many other potential security risks to be aware of, such as

- Weak Passwords: Using weak or easily guessable passwords can make your application vulnerable to brute-force attacks.
- Unpatched Software: Outdated software often contains known security vulnerabilities that attackers can exploit.
- Insecure Configuration: Misconfigured servers or applications can expose vulnerabilities that attackers can leverage.
- Social Engineering: Attackers might use social engineering techniques to trick users into revealing sensitive information or performing actions that compromise security.

Understanding and Mitigating Vulnerabilities

Understanding these common network vulnerabilities is the first step towards building secure applications. The next step is to implement appropriate security measures to mitigate these risks.

This might involve

- Input Validation: Validate all user input to prevent injection attacks.
- Encryption: Use TLS/SSL to encrypt communication between clients and servers.
- Authentication and Authorization: Control access to your application's resources using strong authentication and authorization mechanisms.
- Rate Limiting: Implement rate limiting to prevent denial of service attacks.

- Regular Security Audits: Conduct regular security audits and penetration testing to identify and address potential vulnerabilities.

By staying vigilant and proactive in your security practices, you can build robust and resilient network applications that protect your data and your users from potential threats. Remember, security is an ongoing process, not a one-time event.

9.4 Security Best Practices

Building secure network applications is an ongoing process that requires a combination of vigilance, best practices, and a deep understanding of potential security risks. It's like maintaining a healthy lifestyle – it's not just about taking a vitamin pill once; it's about consistently making good choices and taking preventive measures.

In the world of network security, there are several best practices that can significantly strengthen your application's defenses and protect your data and your users from potential threats. Let's explore these practices:

Use TLS/SSL Encryption

Always encrypt communication between clients and servers using TLS/SSL. This ensures that data in transit is protected from eavesdropping and tampering. Think of it as the fundamental lock on your door, the first line of defense against intruders.

- Obtain a Valid Certificate: Use a valid SSL certificate issued by a trusted Certificate Authority (CA) like Let's Encrypt or Sectigo. Avoid self-signed certificates for production environments, as they don't provide the same level of trust and security.

- Enforce HTTPS: Redirect all HTTP traffic to HTTPS to ensure that all communication is encrypted.
- Stay Up-to-Date: Keep your TLS/SSL libraries and configurations up-to-date to benefit from the latest security patches and improvements.

Validate Input

Never trust user input. Always validate and sanitize any data that comes from external sources, such as user forms, API requests, or file uploads. This helps prevent injection attacks, where attackers try to inject malicious code into your application.

- Sanitize Data: Remove or escape any special characters that could be interpreted as code, such as <, >, &, and quotes.
- Use Parameterized Queries: When interacting with databases, use parameterized queries or prepared statements to prevent SQL injection attacks.
- Validate Data Types and Formats: Ensure that the data received conforms to the expected data types and formats.

Implement Authentication and Authorization

Control access to your application's resources using robust authentication and authorization mechanisms. This ensures that only authorized users can access and modify data.

- Strong Passwords: Enforce strong password policies, requiring users to create passwords that are long, complex, and unique.
- Multi-Factor Authentication (MFA): Consider implementing MFA to add an extra layer of security, requiring users to provide additional verification factors, such as a one-time code or a biometric scan.

- Role-Based Access Control (RBAC): Define roles and permissions to control what actions users can perform based on their roles.

Protect Against DoS Attacks

Denial of Service (DoS) attacks can cripple your application by flooding it with traffic.

Implement measures to mitigate these attacks

- Rate Limiting: Limit the number of requests a client can make within a specific time frame.
- Traffic Filtering: Use firewalls and intrusion detection systems to filter malicious traffic.
- Cloud-Based Protection: Consider using cloud-based DDoS protection services to absorb and deflect large-scale attacks.

Keep Software Updated

Regularly update your software, including your operating system, libraries, and frameworks, to patch security vulnerabilities. Outdated software is a prime target for attackers, as they often contain known vulnerabilities that can be easily exploited.

Follow Secure Coding Practices

Adhere to secure coding practices to prevent common coding errors that can lead to security vulnerabilities.

This includes

- Avoid Hardcoding Secrets: Never hardcode sensitive information, such as API keys or database credentials, in your code. Store them securely in environment variables or configuration files.

- Principle of Least Privilege: Grant users and processes only the minimum necessary permissions to perform their tasks.
- Defense in Depth: Implement multiple layers of security, so that if one layer is compromised, others can still provide protection.

Use Security Tools

Utilize security tools to help you identify and address potential security issues

- Linters: Use linters to analyze your code for potential security vulnerabilities and coding errors.
- Vulnerability Scanners: Use vulnerability scanners to scan your application and dependencies for known vulnerabilities.
- Penetration Testing: Conduct regular penetration testing to simulate real-world attacks and identify weaknesses in your security posture.

Security is an Ongoing Process

Remember that security is not a one-time event; it's an ongoing process. Stay informed about the latest security threats and vulnerabilities, and continuously update your security practices and measures to stay ahead of the curve.

By incorporating these security best practices into your development process and consistently applying them, you can build secure and resilient network applications in Go that protect your data, your users, and your business from potential threats.

Chapter 10: Performance Optimization

In the world of network programming, performance is paramount. Users expect applications to be responsive, snappy, and efficient. A slow or sluggish application can lead to frustration, lost productivity, and even lost revenue. Think of performance optimization as fine-tuning a race car, making it faster, more agile, and more efficient.

In this chapter, we'll explore various techniques for optimizing the performance of your Go network applications. We'll delve into connection pooling, discuss load balancing strategies, explore caching techniques, and touch upon profiling and optimization tools that can help you identify and address performance bottlenecks.

10.1 Connection Pooling

In the world of network programming, efficiency is key. Every millisecond counts, and optimizing your application's performance can make a significant difference in user experience and overall system efficiency. One area where optimization can yield substantial benefits is connection management.

Establishing a new network connection can be a surprisingly time-consuming process. It involves a series of steps, including DNS lookups, TCP handshakes, and potentially SSL/TLS negotiations. These steps add overhead to each connection, and if your application frequently connects to a database, a message queue, or another network service, this overhead can quickly accumulate, leading to performance bottlenecks.

This is where connection pooling comes to the rescue. Think of it as a carpooling system for network connections. Instead of each client creating its own connection to the server, they share a pool of existing connections, reducing the overhead of establishing new connections and improving overall performance.

How Connection Pooling Works

A connection pool is essentially a collection of pre-initialized connections to a server. These connections are kept open and ready to use, eliminating the need to establish a new connection every time a client needs to communicate with the server.

When a client requests a connection, the connection pool checks if there is an available connection in the pool. If there is, it provides the connection to the client. When the client is finished with the connection, it returns it to the pool, making it available for other clients to use.

This "borrow and return" mechanism reduces the overhead of establishing new connections, as the connections are already open and ready to use. It also helps to manage resources efficiently, as the number of open connections is limited to the size of the pool, preventing the server from being overwhelmed by excessive connection requests.

Benefits of Connection Pooling

Connection pooling offers several benefits for network applications

- Reduced Latency: Reusing existing connections eliminates the latency associated with establishing new connections, leading to faster response times for clients.
- Improved Throughput: By reducing the overhead of connection establishment, connection pooling allows the

server to handle more requests per unit of time, increasing overall throughput and efficiency.

- Resource Efficiency: Connection pooling limits the number of open connections, preventing the server from being overwhelmed by excessive connection requests and conserving resources.

Implementing Connection Pooling in Go

Go provides the building blocks for implementing connection pooling through its concurrency primitives and standard library packages. You can use goroutines and channels to manage the pool of connections and synchronize access to them.

Here's a basic example of a connection pool implementation in Go

```
Code snippet

package main


import (

  "fmt"

  "net"

  "sync"

)



// ConnectionPool represents a pool of network
connections
```

```go
type ConnectionPool struct {

  connections chan net.Conn

  mutex        sync.Mutex

}


// NewConnectionPool creates a new connection
pool

func NewConnectionPool(address string, size int)
(*ConnectionPool, error) {

  pool:= &ConnectionPool{

    connections: make(chan net.Conn, size),

  }


  // Initialize the pool with connections

  for i:= 0; i < size; i++ {

    conn, err:= net.Dial("tcp", address)

    if err!= nil {

      return nil, err // Handle error appropriately

    }

    pool.connections <- conn

  }
```

```go
    return pool, nil

}


// Get retrieves a connection from the pool

func (p *ConnectionPool) Get() (net.Conn, error)
{

   select {

   case conn:= <-p.connections:

    return conn, nil

   default:

    return nil, fmt.Errorf("no available
connections")

   }

}


// Put returns a connection to the pool

func (p *ConnectionPool) Put(conn net.Conn) {

  p.mutex.Lock()

  defer p.mutex.Unlock()
```

```go
    select {

    case p.connections <- conn:

    default:

     // Pool is full, close the connection

      conn.Close()

    }

}


func main() {

  // Create a connection pool

  pool, err:= NewConnectionPool("localhost:8080",
10) // Pool of 10 connections

  if err!= nil {

   panic(err)

  }


  // Get a connection from the pool

  conn, err:= pool.Get()

  if err!= nil {

   panic(err)

  }
```

```
// Use the connection

//...


// Return the connection to the pool

pool.Put(conn)

}
```

In this example, the ConnectionPool struct manages a pool of connections using a buffered channel. The Get() method retrieves a connection from the pool, and the Put() method returns a connection to the pool. The sync.Mutex is used to synchronize access to the pool, preventing race conditions when multiple goroutines try to access the pool simultaneously.

Real-World Examples

Connection pooling is widely used in various applications to improve performance and resource utilization

- Database Connections: Database servers typically handle a large number of concurrent connections from applications. Connection pooling helps reduce the overhead of establishing new database connections, improving the performance of database-driven applications.
- Message Queues: Message queues, such as RabbitMQ or Kafka, often handle a high volume of connections from producers and consumers. Connection pooling can improve the efficiency of message processing by reusing connections.
- Web Servers: Web servers that handle a large number of concurrent requests can benefit from connection pooling to

backend services, such as databases or APIs, to reduce latency and improve responsiveness.

By understanding and implementing connection pooling in your Go network applications, you can significantly enhance their performance, efficiency, and scalability, especially in scenarios where frequent connections are required.

10.2 Load Balancing

In the world of high-performance network applications, scalability is key. As your application grows in popularity and usage, a single server might not be enough to handle the increasing traffic and workload. This is where load balancing comes into play.

Think of load balancing as a traffic controller at a busy intersection, directing vehicles into different lanes to ensure smooth traffic flow and prevent congestion. In the context of network applications, a load balancer distributes incoming network traffic across multiple servers, preventing any single server from becoming overwhelmed and ensuring that your application remains responsive and available even under heavy load.

The Benefits of Load Balancing

Load balancing offers several crucial benefits for network applications

- Increased Capacity: By distributing the workload across multiple servers, load balancing increases the overall capacity of your application, allowing it to handle a larger number of users and requests.
- Improved Performance: Load balancing prevents any single server from becoming overloaded, ensuring that requests

are processed quickly and efficiently, leading to better performance and user experience.

- High Availability: If one server fails or becomes unavailable, the load balancer can automatically redirect traffic to other healthy servers, ensuring that your application remains available to users.
- Scalability: Load balancing makes it easier to scale your application horizontally by adding more servers to the pool as needed. This allows you to adapt to growing traffic demands without significant changes to your application's architecture.

Load Balancing Algorithms

The heart of a load balancer lies in its algorithm, which determines how incoming traffic is distributed across the servers.

There are various load balancing algorithms, each with its own characteristics and suitability for different scenarios

- Round Robin: This is a simple and widely used algorithm that distributes requests to servers in a cyclical manner. It's like a merry-go-round, where each server gets a turn to serve a request.
- Least Connections: This algorithm directs requests to the server with the fewest active connections. This ensures that servers with lighter loads receive more requests, optimizing resource utilization.
- IP Hash: This algorithm distributes requests based on the client's IP address. This ensures that requests from the same client are consistently directed to the same server, which can be beneficial for applications that maintain session state or require sticky sessions.

- Weighted Round Robin: This is a variation of the round robin algorithm where each server is assigned a weight, and requests are distributed proportionally to the weights. This allows you to give more powerful or capable servers a larger share of the traffic.
- Random: This algorithm distributes requests randomly across the servers. While simple, it might not be the most efficient or balanced approach.

Load Balancing in Go

While Go itself doesn't provide built-in load balancing features, you can leverage various techniques and tools to implement load balancing for your Go applications:

- Reverse Proxy: A reverse proxy server, such as Nginx or HAProxy, sits in front of your Go application servers and acts as a load balancer. It receives incoming requests and distributes them to the backend servers based on the configured load balancing algorithm. This is a common and effective way to implement load balancing.
- DNS Round Robin: You can configure your DNS records to return multiple IP addresses for your domain. When a client resolves your domain name, it will receive a different IP address each time, effectively distributing traffic across multiple servers. This is a simple approach but might not be as flexible or feature-rich as using a reverse proxy.
- Custom Load Balancer: You can implement your own load balancing logic in your Go application using goroutines and channels. This gives you more control over the load balancing algorithm and allows you to tailor it to your specific needs. However, this approach requires more development effort and might not be as performant or robust as dedicated load balancing solutions.

Real-World Examples

Load balancing is a crucial component of many high-traffic websites and applications

- E-commerce Websites: During peak shopping seasons, e-commerce websites experience a surge in traffic. Load balancing ensures that the website remains responsive and can handle the increased load by distributing traffic across multiple servers.
- Social Media Platforms: Social media platforms like Twitter and Facebook handle millions of concurrent users. Load balancing is essential for distributing the load and ensuring that the platform remains available and responsive.
- Streaming Services: Streaming services like Netflix and Spotify need to handle a large number of users streaming content concurrently. Load balancing ensures smooth playback and prevents buffering issues by distributing the load across multiple servers.
- Cloud Services: Cloud providers like AWS and Google Cloud use load balancing extensively to distribute traffic across their vast infrastructure, ensuring high availability and scalability for their services.

By understanding and implementing load balancing techniques, you can build scalable and resilient Go network applications that can handle increasing traffic demands and provide a seamless experience for your users, even under heavy load.

10.3 Caching Strategies

In the quest for optimal performance, caching emerges as a powerful technique to reduce redundant work and accelerate your Go network applications. Think of caching as storing frequently accessed information in a readily accessible location, like keeping a frequently used cookbook on your kitchen counter instead of retrieving it from the bookshelf every time you need it.

Caching can significantly improve the performance of your applications by reducing the need to perform expensive operations repeatedly, such as fetching data from a database, making external API calls, or performing complex computations. By storing the results of these operations in a cache and reusing them when needed, you can save precious time and resources, leading to faster response times and a smoother user experience.

Types of Caching

There are various types of caching, each with its own characteristics and suitability for different scenarios

- In-Memory Caching: This involves storing cached data in the application's memory. It offers the fastest access times, as the data is readily available in RAM. However, in-memory caching is limited by the amount of available memory and is not persistent across application restarts.
- Disk Caching: This involves storing cached data on disk, typically in files or a dedicated caching system. Disk caching offers more storage capacity than in-memory caching and can persist data across application restarts. However, access times are slower compared to in-memory caching due to the overhead of disk I/O operations.
- CDN Caching: Content Delivery Networks (CDNs) are geographically distributed networks of servers that cache static content, such as images, videos, and CSS files, closer to users. This reduces latency and improves performance for users located far from the origin server.
- Browser Caching: Web browsers can cache static assets, such as images and JavaScript files, locally on the user's machine. This reduces the amount of data that needs to be

downloaded from the server on subsequent visits, improving page load times.

- Server-Side Caching: This involves caching data on the server-side, typically using a dedicated caching layer or a distributed caching system. This can improve the performance of dynamic content by reducing the need to perform database queries or other expensive operations on every request.

Caching Strategies

Choosing the right caching strategy depends on the specific needs of your application and the characteristics of the data being cached.

Some common caching strategies include

- Write-Through Cache: In this strategy, data is written to the cache and the underlying data store (e.g., database) simultaneously. This ensures that the cache is always consistent with the data store, but it can increase write latency.
- Write-Back Cache: In this strategy, data is written only to the cache initially, and the changes are written to the data store later, either periodically or when the cached data is evicted. This improves write performance but introduces the risk of data loss if the cache fails before the changes are written to the data store.
- Cache-Aside: In this strategy, the application first checks the cache for the requested data. If the data is found in the cache, it is returned. Otherwise, the application retrieves the data from the data store, stores it in the cache, and then returns it to the client. This is a common and simple caching strategy.

- Refresh-Ahead: In this strategy, the cache automatically refreshes data before it expires, ensuring that frequently accessed data is always available in the cache.

Implementing Caching in Go

Go provides various ways to implement caching in your applications

- sync.Map: The sync.Map type in Go's sync package provides a thread-safe map implementation that can be used for in-memory caching.
- Third-Party Libraries: Several third-party libraries offer more advanced caching features, such as:
  - go-cache: A simple and lightweight in-memory caching library.
  - groupcache: A distributed caching system that allows applications to share cached data across multiple servers.
  - ristretto: A high-performance, concurrent cache library with support for various eviction policies and features.

Example

Code snippet

```
package main


import (
```

```go
    "fmt"

    "sync"

    "time"

)

var cache sync.Map

func fetchData(key string) (string, error) {

    // Simulate fetching data from a database
    or external API

    fmt.Println("Fetching data from source for
    key:", key)

     time.Sleep(time.Second)

    return fmt.Sprintf("Data for key %s", key),
    nil

}
```

```go
func getCachedData(key string) (string,
error) {

 if value, ok:= cache.Load(key); ok {

  return value.(string), nil

 }

 data, err:= fetchData(key)

 if err!= nil {

  return "", err

 }

 cache.Store(key, data)

 return data, nil

}

func main() {
```

```go
// Get data for key "foo" (will fetch from source)

data, err:= getCachedData("foo")

 if err!= nil {

   panic(err)

 }


fmt.Println("Data:", data)

 // Get data for key "foo" again (will retrieve from cache)

 data, err = getCachedData("foo")

if err!= nil {

   panic(err)

}

  fmt.Println("Data:", data)
```

```
}
```

In this example, the getCachedData function first checks if the data for the given key exists in the cache. If it does, it returns the cached data. Otherwise, it fetches the data from the source, stores it in the cache, and then returns it.

Real-World Examples

Caching is widely used in various applications to improve performance and reduce latency

- Web Servers: Caching frequently accessed web pages or API responses can significantly reduce server load and improve response times.
- Databases: Database caching can reduce the number of queries to the database, improving performance and reducing database load.
- Content Delivery Networks (CDNs): CDNs cache static content closer to users, reducing latency and improving performance for users located far from the origin server.
- Social Media Platforms: Social media platforms cache frequently accessed content, such as user profiles and posts, to reduce database load and improve performance.

By understanding and applying caching strategies in your Go network applications, you can significantly improve their performance, efficiency, and scalability, especially in scenarios where redundant work can be avoided.

10.4 Profiling and Optimization Techniques

In the pursuit of high-performance network applications, profiling and optimization are your trusted allies. Think of profiling as a detective, carefully examining your application's behavior to uncover hidden performance bottlenecks and inefficiencies. Optimization, on the other hand, is the surgeon, skillfully addressing those bottlenecks and fine-tuning your application for optimal speed and efficiency.

Profiling involves collecting data about your application's runtime behavior, such as CPU usage, memory allocation, and network activity. This data provides valuable insights into where your application is spending its time and resources, allowing you to pinpoint areas that need optimization.

Optimization, then, is the process of applying various techniques and strategies to improve the performance of those identified bottlenecks. It might involve refining algorithms, reducing memory allocations, minimizing I/O operations, or utilizing concurrency effectively.

Profiling Tools in Go

Go provides powerful built-in tools for profiling your applications

- pprof: This is a versatile tool that can generate and analyze various types of profiles, including CPU profiles, memory profiles, and block profiles. It can also visualize the profiles, helping you understand the call graphs and identify hotspots in your code.
- To use pprof, you first need to enable profiling in your application by importing the net/http/pprof package and registering its handlers:

Code snippet

```
import _ "net/http/pprof"


func main() {

    //... your application code...


    go func() {

log.Println(http.ListenAndServe("localhost:6060",
nil))

    }()


    //... rest of your application code...

}
```

This will start a profiling server on localhost:6060, allowing you to access various profiling endpoints. You can then use the go tool pprof command to analyze the profiles.

go test -bench: This command allows you to run benchmarks and measure the performance of specific functions or code blocks. Benchmarks are special functions that are executed repeatedly to measure their execution time.

To write a benchmark, create a function with the name BenchmarkXxx (where Xxx is the name of the function you're benchmarking) and use the b *testing.B parameter to control the benchmark loop:

Code snippet

```
func BenchmarkMyFunction(b *testing.B) {

    for i:= 0; i < b.N; i++ {

        MyFunction() // Call the function you're
benchmarking

    }

}
```

You can then run the benchmark using go test -bench..

Optimization Techniques

Once you've identified performance bottlenecks through profiling, you can apply various optimization techniques to improve your application's performance:

- Reduce Memory Allocations: Memory allocations can be expensive, especially if they happen frequently. Minimize memory allocations by reusing objects, using more efficient data structures, or pre-allocating memory when possible.
- Optimize Algorithms and Data Structures: Choose algorithms and data structures that are well-suited for the task at hand. Consider the time and space complexity of different algorithms and choose the ones that offer the best performance for your specific needs.
- Minimize I/O Operations: I/O operations, such as disk reads and writes or network requests, can be slow. Minimize these operations by caching frequently accessed data, using efficient I/O libraries, or performing I/O operations concurrently.
- Use Concurrency Effectively: Utilize goroutines and channels to perform tasks concurrently, taking advantage of multiple processor cores and improving responsiveness. However, be mindful of the overhead of context switching and synchronization when using concurrency.
- Optimize for the Specific Use Case: Consider the specific use case and performance requirements of your application. Optimize for the most critical operations and focus on the areas that have the biggest impact on overall performance.

Real-World Examples

Profiling and optimization are essential practices in many high-performance applications

- Web Servers: Web servers need to handle a large number of concurrent requests efficiently. Profiling and optimization techniques can help identify and address bottlenecks in request handling, data processing, and network communication.

- Databases: Database systems are highly optimized for performance. Profiling and optimization techniques are used to improve query execution, indexing, and data storage.
- Game Engines: Game engines need to render graphics, simulate physics, and handle user input in real-time. Profiling and optimization are crucial for achieving smooth frame rates and responsive gameplay.
- High-Performance Computing (HPC): HPC applications often involve complex computations and large datasets. Profiling and optimization techniques are used to maximize performance and utilize resources efficiently.

By incorporating profiling and optimization into your development process, you can ensure that your Go network applications are not only functional and correct but also performant and efficient. Remember, performance optimization is an iterative process, and continuous monitoring and improvement are key to maintaining optimal performance as your application evolves and grows.

Chapter 11: Testing and Debugging Network Applications

In the world of software development, testing and debugging are your trusty companions, guiding you towards a robust and reliable application. Think of testing as a series of rigorous quality checks, ensuring that your code behaves as expected under various conditions. Debugging, on the other hand, is the detective work you undertake when things go wrong, helping you identify and resolve those pesky bugs that can cause unexpected behavior or crashes.

In this chapter, we'll explore the essential aspects of testing and debugging network applications in Go. We'll delve into unit testing techniques for network code, discuss integration testing strategies, explore network monitoring tools, and touch upon debugging techniques that can help you pinpoint and resolve issues in your network applications.

11.1 Unit Testing Network Code

Testing is a cornerstone of good software development, and network applications are no exception. In this section, we'll focus on unit testing, a critical practice that involves testing individual units of your code in isolation to ensure they function correctly. Think of it like testing the individual components of a car—the engine, the brakes, the transmission—before putting them all together to ensure the car runs smoothly.

In the context of network applications, unit testing might involve testing functions that handle network connections, send and receive data, or process network protocols. These tests help you catch bugs early in the development process, ensuring that each component of your network application works as expected before you integrate them into a larger system.

Challenges of Unit Testing Network Code

Testing network code presents unique challenges compared to testing other types of code.

This is primarily because network code often relies on external dependencies, such as

- Network Connectivity: Your code might depend on a stable network connection to communicate with remote servers or services.
- Remote Servers: Your tests might need to interact with external servers or APIs that might not always be available or might have varying responses.
- Databases: If your network application interacts with a database, your tests might need to access and manipulate the database, which can introduce complexity and dependencies.

These external dependencies can make it difficult to create reliable and repeatable unit tests. Network conditions can fluctuate, remote servers can be unavailable, and databases can have varying states, all of which can affect the outcome of your tests.

Strategies for Effective Unit Testing

To overcome these challenges and write effective unit tests for your network code, consider the following strategies

- Mocking: Mocking involves creating fake or simulated versions of external dependencies. This allows you to isolate the code under test and control its interactions with the outside world. Instead of relying on a real network connection, you can use a mock object that simulates the network behavior, allowing you to test different scenarios, such as successful connections, connection failures, or specific data responses.

- Go provides several libraries for creating mocks, such as testify/mock and go-mock. These libraries allow you to define mock objects that implement the same interfaces as your real dependencies, giving you fine-grained control over their behavior during testing.

- Dependency Injection: Dependency injection is a design pattern where dependencies are passed into your functions or methods as parameters rather than being created directly within the code. This makes it easier to swap out real dependencies with mocks during testing.

- For example, instead of creating a network connection directly within your function, you could pass the connection as a parameter:

Code snippet

```go
func sendMessage(conn net.Conn, message string)
error {

    //... use the conn object to send the
message...

}
```

This allows you to pass a real network connection in production and a mock connection during testing.

- Test Doubles: Test doubles are objects that stand in for real dependencies during testing. They can be used to simulate specific behaviors or responses, allowing you to test different scenarios and edge cases. There are various types of test doubles, including:
  - Dummies: Objects that are passed around but never actually used.
  - Stubs: Objects that provide canned answers to calls made during the test.
  - Mocks: Objects that are pre-programmed with expectations, which form a specification of the calls they are expected to receive.

Example

Let's say you have a function that retrieves data from a remote API

Code snippet

```
func fetchData(url string) (byte, error) {

    resp, err:= http.Get(url)

    if err!= nil {

        return nil, err

    }

    defer resp.Body.Close()


    return ioutil.ReadAll(resp.Body)
```

```
}
```

To unit test this function without actually making a network request, you could create a mock HTTP client

```
Code snippet

type mockHTTPClient struct {

    response *http.Response

    err       error

}



func (m *mockHTTPClient) Get(url string)
(*http.Response, error) {

    return m.response, m.err

}



func TestFetchData(t *testing.T) {

    mockResponse:= &http.Response{

        StatusCode: http.StatusOK,

        Body:
ioutil.NopCloser(bytes.NewBufferString(`{"message
": "Hello, world!"}`)),

    }

    mockClient:= &mockHTTPClient{response:
mockResponse}
```

```go
    data, err:=
fetchData("https://example.com/api", mockClient)
// Inject the mock client

    if err!= nil {

        t.Errorf("Unexpected error: %v", err)

    }



    expected:=byte(`{"message": "Hello,
world!"}`)

    if!bytes.Equal(data, expected) {

        t.Errorf("Expected data '%s', got '%s'",
expected, data)

    }

}
```

In this example, the mockHTTPClient struct implements the http.Client interface and provides a pre-defined response. The TestFetchData function injects the mock client into the fetchData function and then checks if the returned data matches the expected response.

By utilizing these strategies and tools, you can effectively unit test your network code, ensuring that each component functions correctly in isolation and laying a solid foundation for building reliable and robust network applications.

11.2 Integration Testing

While unit tests focus on individual components in isolation, integration tests take a broader perspective, examining how different parts of your application work together as a cohesive whole. Think of it like assembling the car after testing its individual components. You want to make sure that the engine, brakes, transmission, and other parts interact correctly and produce the desired outcome—a smoothly running vehicle.

In network applications, integration testing is crucial for uncovering issues that might not be apparent during unit testing. It helps you verify that your application interacts correctly with external systems, such as databases, message queues, or external APIs. It also helps you identify potential problems with network connectivity, latency, or configuration.

Benefits of Integration Testing

Integration testing offers several benefits

- Catches Compatibility Issues: It helps identify compatibility issues between different components or versions of your application. For example, if you upgrade a database library, integration tests can ensure that your application still interacts correctly with the database.
- Uncovers Configuration Errors: It can reveal configuration errors that might affect the interaction between components. For example, if your application is misconfigured to connect to the wrong database server, integration tests will likely catch this error.
- Exposes Network Issues: It can expose network-related issues, such as latency or connectivity problems, that might affect performance or reliability.
- Increases Confidence: Successful integration tests increase your confidence in the overall functionality and stability of

your application, as they demonstrate that the different parts work together as expected.

Strategies for Effective Integration Testing

To conduct effective integration testing, consider the following strategies

- Test Environments: Set up dedicated test environments that closely resemble your production environment. This ensures that your tests are representative of real-world scenarios and helps you catch environment-specific issues.
- Realistic Test Data: Use realistic test data that mimics the data your application will encounter in production. This helps you identify potential issues with data handling, validation, or transformation.
- Automated Tests: Automate your integration tests to ensure that they are run regularly and consistently. This helps you catch regressions early and maintain the quality of your application over time.
- Focus on Critical Interactions: Prioritize testing the most critical interactions between your application and external systems. For example, if your application relies heavily on a database, focus on testing the database interactions thoroughly.

Types of Integration Tests

There are different types of integration tests, each with its own focus and scope

- Big Bang Integration: This involves integrating all components at once and testing the entire system as a whole. While this can be useful for final integration testing, it can be difficult to pinpoint the source of errors if they occur.
- Incremental Integration: This involves integrating components gradually, testing each integration step along the way. This makes it easier to identify the source of errors and can be more efficient for larger systems.
- Top-Down Integration: This involves integrating components from the top down, starting with the user interface and working down to the lower-level components. This can be useful for testing the user experience and ensuring that the high-level functionality works as expected.
- Bottom-Up Integration: This involves integrating components from the bottom up, starting with the lowest-level components and working up to the user interface. This can be useful for testing the core functionality and ensuring that the underlying components are working correctly.

Real-World Examples

Integration testing is crucial in various real-world scenarios

- Microservices: In microservices architectures, where applications are composed of multiple independent services, integration testing is essential for ensuring that the services can communicate and interact correctly.

- E-commerce Platforms: Integration testing is used to verify that the different components of an e-commerce platform, such as the product catalog, shopping cart, and payment gateway, work together seamlessly.
- Data Pipelines: Integration testing is used to test the flow of data through a data pipeline, ensuring that data is extracted, transformed, and loaded correctly between different systems.
- Cloud Applications: Integration testing is used to test the interaction between cloud applications and cloud services, such as databases, message queues, and storage services.

By incorporating integration testing into your development process, you can ensure that the different parts of your Go network application work together harmoniously, providing a reliable and robust experience for your users. Remember, integration testing is not just about testing the individual components; it's about testing the system as a whole, ensuring that all the pieces fit together and function as expected.

11.3 Network Monitoring Tools

In the dynamic world of network applications, where performance and reliability are paramount, network monitoring tools are your eyes and ears, providing valuable insights into the health and behavior of your applications. Think of them as the instruments on the dashboard of your car, giving you real-time information about speed, fuel level, engine temperature, and other vital signs.

Network monitoring tools allow you to observe network traffic, track performance metrics, identify bottlenecks, and troubleshoot issues. They provide a window into the inner workings of your network applications, helping you ensure smooth operation and optimal performance.

Let's explore some essential network monitoring tools that can be invaluable for developers and system administrators working with Go network applications:

tcpdump: This is a powerful command-line tool that allows you to capture and analyze network traffic. It's like a surveillance camera for your network, capturing packets as they flow through your network interfaces. You can use tcpdump to filter traffic based on various criteria, such as source and destination IP addresses, ports, or protocols. This allows you to focus on specific traffic patterns and identify potential issues.

Wireshark: Wireshark is a graphical network protocol analyzer that provides a more user-friendly interface for capturing and inspecting network traffic. It allows you to visualize network packets in detail, analyze their contents, and identify potential problems. Wireshark supports a wide range of protocols and provides powerful filtering and analysis capabilities.

Prometheus: Prometheus is an open-source monitoring system and time series database. It can collect metrics from your Go applications, including network-related metrics such as request latency, error rates, and connection counts. You can then use Prometheus's query language to analyze these metrics, create dashboards, and set up alerts for specific conditions.

Grafana: Grafana is a popular open-source data visualization and monitoring tool. It can be used to create interactive dashboards and visualizations based on data from various sources, including Prometheus. Grafana allows you to create customized dashboards that display key network metrics, providing a comprehensive view of your application's performance and health.

Go-Specific Tools

In addition to these general-purpose network monitoring tools, there are also Go-specific tools and libraries that can be helpful for monitoring your Go network applications:

- net/http/pprof: This package provides profiling data for your Go applications, including network-related metrics such as the number of active goroutines, the number of open connections, and the amount of network I/O. You can access this data through a web interface or programmatically using the pprof tool.
- expvar: This package provides a standardized way to expose metrics from your Go applications. You can use expvar to publish network-related metrics, such as request counts, latency histograms, and error rates, making them accessible for monitoring and analysis.

Real-World Applications

Network monitoring tools are essential for various real-world scenarios

- Troubleshooting Network Issues: When network problems arise, monitoring tools can help you identify the source of the problem, whether it's a slow connection, a misconfigured server, or a network outage.
- Performance Optimization: By monitoring network metrics, you can identify performance bottlenecks and optimize your application to reduce latency, improve throughput, and enhance the user experience.
- Security Monitoring: Network monitoring tools can help you detect and respond to security threats, such as suspicious traffic patterns or denial-of-service attacks.

- Capacity Planning: By monitoring network usage trends, you can plan for future capacity needs and ensure that your infrastructure can handle increasing traffic demands.

By incorporating network monitoring tools into your development and operations workflow, you gain valuable insights into the behavior and performance of your Go network applications. These tools empower you to proactively identify and address issues, optimize performance, and ensure the smooth and reliable operation of your applications.

11.4 Debugging Techniques

Debugging is an essential skill for any programmer, especially when dealing with the complexities of network applications. Think of debugging as detective work, where you carefully examine the clues and evidence to uncover the root cause of a problem. It's the process of identifying and resolving errors, unexpected behavior, or crashes in your code.

Debugging network applications can be particularly challenging, as the interactions between different components and systems can be complex and unpredictable. However, with the right tools and techniques, you can effectively track down and resolve issues, ensuring that your network applications run smoothly and reliably.

Essential Debugging Techniques

Let's explore some essential debugging techniques that can help you diagnose and resolve issues in your Go network applications

- Logging: Logging is one of the most fundamental debugging techniques. It involves recording events, errors, and other relevant information during the execution of your application. This log provides a valuable trail of breadcrumbs that can help you understand the application's behavior and pinpoint the source of problems.

- Go provides a built-in logging package (log) that allows you to write log messages to various outputs, such as the console, a file, or a network stream. You can use different log levels, such as debug, info, warning, and error, to categorize messages and filter them based on their severity.
- Effective logging involves:
  - Logging Relevant Information: Include relevant information in your log messages, such as timestamps, function names, and variable values.
  - Using Different Log Levels: Use different log levels to distinguish between informational messages, warnings, and errors.
  - Logging Strategically: Avoid excessive logging, which can clutter your logs and make it harder to find relevant information. Focus on logging key events and potential error conditions.
- Debugging Tools: Debuggers are powerful tools that allow you to step through your code line by line, inspect variables, and set breakpoints to pause execution at specific points. This gives you a fine-grained view of your application's state and helps you identify the exact point where an error occurs.
- Go has several excellent debuggers available, including:
  - Delve: A popular debugger specifically designed for Go. It provides a command-line interface and integration with various editors and IDEs.
  - GDB: The GNU Debugger, a versatile debugger that supports multiple languages, including Go.
- Using a debugger involves:
  - Setting Breakpoints: Pause execution at specific lines of code to inspect the application's state.

- Stepping Through Code: Execute your code line by line, observing the flow of execution and the values of variables.
- Inspecting Variables: Examine the values of variables at different points in the execution to understand how they change and identify potential issues.
- Network Analyzers: Network analyzers, such as tcpdump or Wireshark, allow you to capture and analyze network traffic. This can be invaluable for debugging network-related issues, such as slow connections, packet loss, or protocol errors.
- Using a network analyzer involves:
  - Capturing Network Traffic: Capture network packets as they flow through your network interfaces.
  - Filtering Traffic: Filter the captured traffic based on criteria such as source and destination IP addresses, ports, or protocols.
  - Inspecting Packets: Inspect the contents of individual packets to understand the communication between your application and other systems.

Debugging Strategies

Effective debugging often involves a combination of techniques and strategies

- Reproduce the Error: The first step in debugging is to reproduce the error reliably. This allows you to consistently observe the problem and test potential solutions.
- Isolate the Problem: Try to isolate the problem to a specific part of your code or a specific interaction with an external system. This helps you narrow down the search for the root cause.

- Use the Scientific Method: Formulate hypotheses about the cause of the error and test them systematically. Use logging, debugging tools, and network analyzers to gather evidence and refine your hypotheses.
- Simplify the Code: If the code is complex, try to simplify it or break it down into smaller, more manageable parts to make it easier to debug.
- Ask for Help: Don't hesitate to ask for help from colleagues or online communities. Sometimes a fresh perspective can help you see the problem in a new light.

Real-World Examples

Debugging is an essential skill in various real-world scenarios

- Troubleshooting API Issues: When integrating with a third-party API, debugging can help you identify issues with API requests, responses, or authentication.
- Resolving Database Errors: Debugging can help you pinpoint the cause of database errors, such as connection failures, query errors, or data inconsistencies.
- Analyzing Network Performance: Debugging tools and network analyzers can help you identify network bottlenecks, latency issues, or packet loss.
- Diagnosing Application Crashes: Debuggers can help you analyze core dumps and trace the execution flow leading up to a crash, helping you identify the root cause.

By mastering these debugging techniques and utilizing the tools available in Go and its ecosystem, you can effectively diagnose and resolve issues in your network applications, ensuring that they run smoothly, reliably, and provide a positive experience for your users. Remember, debugging is not just about fixing bugs; it's about understanding your code, improving its quality, and building confidence in its reliability.

Chapter 12: Deploying Network Applications

You've built a robust, high-performance network application in Go. Now, it's time to share it with the world! Deploying your application is the process of making it accessible to users, whether it's a web server, an API, or a backend service. Think of it as launching your carefully crafted ship into the vast ocean of the internet.

Deploying network applications can be a complex process, involving various considerations such as server infrastructure, scalability, security, and monitoring. In this chapter, we'll explore different deployment strategies, focusing on cloud deployment, containerization, and traditional server deployments.

12.1 Cloud Deployment (AWS, GCP, Azure)

Cloud computing has revolutionized the way we build, deploy, and manage applications. It's like having access to a vast, on-demand IT infrastructure, allowing you to scale your applications effortlessly, pay only for what you use, and focus on innovation rather than managing servers.

For deploying Go network applications, cloud platforms like Amazon Web Services (AWS), Google Cloud Platform (GCP), and Microsoft Azure offer a compelling proposition. They provide a wide array of services and tools that simplify deployment, enhance scalability, and ensure high availability.

Think of these cloud platforms as giant, well-equipped data centers that you can tap into whenever you need. They provide the infrastructure, the services, and the management tools, allowing you to focus on building and deploying your applications without the hassle of managing physical servers or complex infrastructure.

Benefits of Cloud Deployment

Cloud deployment offers several compelling benefits for Go network applications

- Scalability: Cloud platforms are designed for scalability. You can easily scale your applications up or down based on demand, adding or removing resources such as compute power, storage, and network bandwidth as needed. This allows you to handle traffic spikes, accommodate growth, and optimize costs.
- Cost-Effectiveness: Cloud computing follows a pay-as-you-go model. You only pay for the resources you consume, making it a cost-effective option, especially for applications with variable workloads or unpredictable traffic patterns.
- Reliability: Cloud providers invest heavily in infrastructure and redundancy, ensuring high availability for your applications. They have multiple data centers, backup systems, and disaster recovery mechanisms in place to ensure that your applications remain accessible even in case of hardware failures or other disruptions.
- Global Reach: Cloud providers have data centers located around the world. This allows you to deploy your applications closer to your users, reducing latency and improving performance. You can also choose regions that offer the best cost or compliance characteristics for your application.
- Ease of Management: Cloud platforms provide a wealth of tools and services for managing your applications, including monitoring, logging, security, and automation. This simplifies operations and allows you to focus on building and improving your applications.

Deploying Go Applications on Cloud Platforms

Each cloud provider offers a variety of services for deploying applications, catering to different needs and deployment models

- Virtual Machines (VMs): VMs are like emulated computers in the cloud. You can choose a VM with the operating system and specifications that suit your application, install your Go application and its dependencies, and run it as a standalone server. This gives you a high degree of control over the environment but requires more manual configuration and management.
- Containers: Containers, such as Docker, provide a lightweight and portable way to package and deploy applications. You can containerize your Go application and deploy it on container orchestration platforms like Kubernetes, which are offered by all major cloud providers. Containers offer greater efficiency and portability compared to VMs.
- Serverless Functions: Serverless functions, such as AWS Lambda or Google Cloud Functions, allow you to run your code without managing servers. You can deploy your Go functions as serverless functions and trigger them in response to events, such as HTTP requests or messages from a queue. This is a highly scalable and cost-effective option for event-driven applications.

Cloud Deployment Tools

Cloud providers offer a range of tools and services to streamline the deployment and management of your applications

- Command-Line Interfaces (CLIs): CLIs provide a way to interact with cloud services from your terminal, allowing you to automate deployment and management tasks. AWS provides the AWS CLI, GCP provides the gcloud CLI, and Azure provides the Azure CLI.
- Web Consoles: Web consoles provide a graphical interface for managing your cloud resources and deployments. You can use the web console to create VMs, configure networks, monitor resources, and manage deployments.
- Infrastructure-as-Code (IaC) Tools: IaC tools, such as Terraform or AWS CloudFormation, allow you to define your infrastructure in code, making it easier to manage, version, and automate deployments. This approach promotes consistency and reproducibility, reducing the risk of errors and configuration drift.

Choosing the Right Cloud Deployment Service

The choice of which cloud deployment service to use depends on various factors

- Application Requirements: Consider the specific needs of your application, such as scalability, performance, and security requirements.
- Cost: Evaluate the cost of different services, including compute, storage, and network costs.
- Expertise: Assess your team's familiarity with different cloud platforms and services.

- Deployment Model: Choose a service that aligns with your preferred deployment model, whether it's VMs, containers, or serverless functions.

By carefully considering these factors and understanding the different cloud deployment options available, you can choose the best approach for deploying your Go network applications, leveraging the scalability, reliability, and cost-effectiveness of the cloud.

12.2 Containerization (Docker, Kubernetes)

In the world of software deployment, containerization has emerged as a game-changer. Think of containers as lightweight, portable packages that encapsulate your application and all its dependencies, ensuring that it runs consistently regardless of the underlying infrastructure. It's like having a self-contained travel suitcase that contains everything you need for your trip, no matter where you go.

Containers provide a consistent and isolated environment for your application, eliminating the "it works on my machine" problem and making it easier to move applications between different environments, such as development, testing, and production. This consistency and portability have made containers a popular choice for deploying modern applications, including Go network applications.

Docker

Docker is a leading containerization platform that allows you to build, ship, and run containerized applications. It provides a simple and efficient way to package your Go application and its dependencies into a container image, which can then be run on any system that has Docker installed.

Think of Docker as the shipping company that handles your travel suitcase. It provides the tools and infrastructure for packaging your application and its dependencies into a standardized container image, transporting it to its destination, and running it in a secure and isolated environment.

Key Concepts in Docker

- Dockerfile: A Dockerfile is a text file that contains instructions for building a Docker image. It specifies the base image[1] to use, the application code to copy, the dependencies to install, and other configurations. It's like the packing list for your travel suitcase, specifying what needs to be included.
- Docker Image: A Docker image is a read-only template that contains your application and its dependencies. It's like a snapshot of your travel suitcase, ready to be used to create running containers.
- Docker Container: A Docker container is a running instance of a Docker image. It's like opening your travel suitcase and using its contents at your destination.

Building and Running a Docker Container

To containerize your Go application with Docker, you typically follow these steps

1. Create a Dockerfile: Define the instructions for building your Docker image in a Dockerfile.
2. Build the Image: Use the docker build command to build the Docker image based on your Dockerfile.

3. Run the Container: Use the docker run command to create and run a container from your Docker image.

Example Dockerfile for a Go Application

```
Dockerfile

FROM golang:latest # Use the latest Go base image


WORKDIR /app # Set the working directory inside
the container


COPY go.mod./ # Copy the Go module files

COPY go.sum./

RUN go mod download # Download the dependencies


COPY.. # Copy the application code


RUN go build -o main. # Build the Go application


CMD ["./main"] # Set the command to run the
application
```

This Dockerfile uses the latest official Go image as the base image, sets the working directory to /app, copies the Go module files (go.mod and go.sum), downloads the dependencies using go mod download, copies the rest of the application code, builds the application using go build, and finally sets the command to run the application when the container starts.

Kubernetes

While Docker provides the tools for building and running individual containers, Kubernetes takes it a step further by orchestrating and managing containers at scale. Think of Kubernetes as the travel agent that handles all the logistics of your trip, ensuring that you have the right transportation, accommodation, and itinerary.

Kubernetes allows you to deploy your Docker containers across a cluster of machines, ensuring high availability, scalability, and fault tolerance.

It provides features such as

- Automated Deployment: Kubernetes automates the deployment of your containers, ensuring that they are scheduled and run on the appropriate nodes in the cluster.
- Scaling: Kubernetes can automatically scale your application by adding or removing containers based on demand, ensuring that your application can handle varying workloads.
- Self-Healing: Kubernetes monitors the health of your containers and automatically restarts or replaces any containers that fail, ensuring high availability for your application.
- Service Discovery: Kubernetes provides service discovery, allowing your containers to easily find and communicate with each other.
- Rolling Updates: Kubernetes supports rolling updates, allowing you to deploy new versions of your application without downtime.

Deploying Go Applications with Kubernetes

Deploying a Go application with Kubernetes typically involves

1. Containerizing your application: Package your application and its dependencies into a Docker image.
2. Creating a Kubernetes Deployment: Define a Kubernetes Deployment object that describes how your application should be deployed, including the Docker image to use, the number of replicas, and other configurations.
3. Creating a Kubernetes Service: Define a Kubernetes Service object that exposes your application to the network, allowing clients to access it.

Benefits of Containerization

Containerization offers several benefits for deploying Go network applications

- Portability: Containerized applications can be easily moved between different environments, making it easier to develop, test, and deploy applications consistently.
- Consistency: Containers provide a consistent runtime environment, ensuring that your application runs the same way regardless of the underlying infrastructure.
- Efficiency: Containers are lightweight and share the host operating system's kernel, making them more efficient than virtual machines.
- Scalability: Container orchestration platforms like Kubernetes make it easy to scale your applications by adding or removing containers as needed.

By embracing containerization with Docker and Kubernetes, you can streamline your deployment process, improve the scalability and reliability of your Go network applications, and focus on building innovative and high-performance applications.

12.3 Server Deployment Strategies

Deploying your Go network application involves choosing the right strategy for your specific needs and infrastructure. It's like selecting the best transportation method for a journey - you'd consider factors like distance, cost, speed, and comfort before deciding whether to walk, bike, drive, or fly.

Similarly, when deploying your application, you need to consider factors such as scalability, performance, cost, security, and control.

Let's explore some common server deployment strategies

Traditional Server Deployment

This is the classic approach, where you deploy your application on physical or virtual servers that you manage yourself. It's like owning your own car - you have full control over its maintenance, customization, and upgrades, but you're also responsible for all the associated costs and complexities.

- Physical Servers: You can purchase and maintain your own physical servers, giving you complete control over the hardware and software. This offers the highest level of customization and performance but also requires significant investment in hardware, infrastructure, and maintenance.
- Virtual Private Servers (VPS): VPS are virtualized instances of physical servers, providing a more cost-effective and flexible option. You still have a good degree of control over the environment, but the underlying hardware is managed by the hosting provider.

Benefits of Traditional Server Deployment

- Control: You have full control over the server environment, including the operating system, software, and configurations.
- Customization: You can customize the server to meet your specific needs, optimizing it for performance, security, or specific applications.
- Cost-Effective for Stable Workloads: For applications with stable and predictable workloads, traditional server deployment can be cost-effective, as you pay a fixed cost for the server regardless of usage.

Challenges of Traditional Server Deployment

- Maintenance: You're responsible for maintaining the server, including security updates, software upgrades, and troubleshooting.
- Scalability: Scaling can be more complex and time-consuming, requiring manual intervention to add or remove servers.
- Upfront Investment: Physical servers require a significant upfront investment in hardware and infrastructure.

Bare Metal Deployment

Bare metal deployment involves deploying your application directly on physical servers without a virtualization layer. It's like riding a motorcycle - you have a direct connection to the engine and the road, providing the best possible performance and control.

This approach offers the highest performance and efficiency, as there's no overhead from virtualization. However, it also requires specialized hardware and expertise to manage.

Benefits of Bare Metal Deployment

- Performance: Bare metal servers offer the best possible performance, as there's no overhead from virtualization.
- Control: You have complete control over the hardware and software, allowing for maximum customization and optimization.
- Security: Bare metal servers can offer enhanced security, as there's no shared infrastructure or virtualization layer that could be exploited.

Challenges of Bare Metal Deployment

- Cost: Bare metal servers can be expensive, especially for high-performance configurations.
- Maintenance: You're responsible for all aspects of server maintenance, including hardware and software.
- Scalability: Scaling can be more complex, requiring the purchase and provisioning of new physical servers.

Hybrid Deployment

Hybrid deployment involves a combination of cloud deployment and traditional server deployment. It's like using a combination of transportation methods for a journey - you might take a train for part of the trip and then rent a car for the remaining distance.

This approach allows you to leverage the benefits of both cloud and traditional deployments, such as the scalability and cost-effectiveness of the cloud and the control and customization of traditional servers.

Benefits of Hybrid Deployment

- Flexibility: You can choose the best deployment option for each component of your application, balancing cost, performance, and control.
- Scalability: You can leverage the scalability of the cloud for components that require it, while maintaining control over critical components on your own servers.
- Cost Optimization: You can optimize costs by using the cloud for variable workloads and traditional servers for stable workloads.

Challenges of Hybrid Deployment

- Complexity: Managing a hybrid environment can be more complex, requiring expertise in both cloud and traditional deployments.
- Integration: Integrating different environments can be challenging, requiring careful planning and configuration.

Deployment Tools

Various tools can help you with server deployment, regardless of the chosen strategy

- Ansible: An automation tool that allows you to automate server configuration and application deployment. It uses a simple, agentless architecture and can manage both physical and virtual servers.
- Chef: Another automation tool that uses a "recipe" based approach to server configuration and deployment. It provides a domain-specific language (DSL) for defining infrastructure and applications.

- Puppet: A configuration management tool that allows you to define and manage the state of your servers. It uses a declarative language to specify the desired state of your infrastructure.

Choosing the Right Deployment Strategy

The best server deployment strategy for your Go network application depends on various factors

- Application Requirements: Consider the specific needs of your application, such as scalability, performance, and security requirements.
- Cost: Evaluate the cost of different deployment options, including infrastructure, management, and maintenance.
- Expertise: Assess your team's familiarity with different deployment technologies and platforms.
- Control: Determine the level of control you need over the infrastructure and deployment process.

By carefully considering these factors and understanding the different deployment strategies available, you can make an informed decision that aligns with your application's needs and your organizational goals.

Conclusion

Congratulations on reaching the end of this journey into the world of Go network programming! You've come a long way, from understanding the fundamental concepts of networking to building sophisticated, high-performance applications. You've learned how to wield the power of Go's concurrency model, handle various network protocols, work with different data formats, and secure your applications against potential threats.

As you venture forth into the vast landscape of network programming, remember the key principles and practices we've explored:

- Embrace Concurrency: Go's goroutines and channels are your allies in building efficient and scalable network applications. Utilize them to handle multiple connections, process data concurrently, and build responsive systems.
- Master the Protocols: Familiarize yourself with the common network protocols, such as TCP, UDP, HTTP, and WebSockets. Understand their strengths and weaknesses, and choose the right protocol for your specific needs.
- Structure Your Data: Choose appropriate data formats, such as JSON, XML, or Protobuf, to structure and exchange data efficiently and reliably.
- Prioritize Security: Implement robust security measures, such as TLS/SSL encryption, authentication, and authorization, to protect your applications and your users' data from potential threats.
- Optimize for Performance: Utilize techniques like connection pooling, load balancing, and caching to optimize the performance of your applications and provide a smooth user experience.
- Test Thoroughly: Employ unit tests, integration tests, and network monitoring tools to ensure the quality, reliability, and performance of your applications.

- Debug Effectively: Master debugging techniques and tools to identify and resolve issues efficiently, ensuring the smooth operation of your applications.
- Deploy Strategically: Choose the right deployment strategy, whether it's cloud deployment, containerization, or traditional server deployment, based on your application's needs and your organizational goals.

The world of network programming is constantly evolving, with new technologies and challenges emerging all the time. Stay curious, keep learning, and continue to explore the vast possibilities that Go offers for building innovative and high-performance network applications.

As you embark on your future projects, remember that the Go community is a valuable resource. Share your knowledge, contribute to open-source projects, and engage with other Go developers to learn and grow together.

Thank you for joining me on this journey. I hope this book has equipped you with the knowledge and skills you need to build amazing things with Go and the power of networking. Now go forth and create!

www.ingramcontent.com/pod-product-compliance
Lightning Source LLC
LaVergne TN
LVHW081521050326
832903LV00025B/1573